W9-CCB-664

The 21 Most Encouraging Promises of the Bible

Dave Earley

© 2006 by David Earley

ISBN 1-59789-043-X

All rights reserved. No part of this publication may be reproduced or transmitted for commercial purposes, except for brief quotations in printed reviews, without written permission of the publisher.

Churches and other noncommercial interests may reproduce portions of this book without the express written permission of Barbour Publishing, provided that the text does not exceed 500 words or 5 percent of the entire book, whichever is less, and that the text is not material quoted from another publisher. When reproducing text from this book, include the following credit line: "From *The 21 Most Encouraging Promises of the Bible*, published by Barbour Publishing, Inc. Used by permission."

All Scripture quotations, unless otherwise indicated, are taken from the Holy Bible, New International Version®. niv®. Copyright © 1973, 1978, 1984 by International Bible Society. Used by permission of Zondervan. All rights reserved.

Scripture quotations marked nasb are taken from the New American Standard Bible, © 1960, 1962, 1963, 1968, 1971, 1972, 1973, 1975, 1977 by The Lockman Foundation. Used by permission.

Scripture quotations marked nkjv are taken from the New King James Version. Copyright © 1979, 1980, 1982 by Thomas Nelson, Inc. Used by permission. All rights reserved.

Scripture quotations marked The Message are taken from *The Message*. Copyright © by Eugene H. Peterson 1993, 1994, 1995, 1996, 2000, 2001, 2002. Used by permission of NavPress Publishing Group.

Scripture quotations marked amp are from the Amplified New Testament, © 1954, 1958, 1987 by the Lockman Foundation. Used by permission.

Cover design by Garborg Design Works, Inc.
Cover photo by Loren Garborg

The author is represented by literary agent Les Stobbe.

Published by Barbour Publishing, Inc., P.O. Box 719, Uhrichsville, Ohio 44683
www.barbourbooks.com

Our mission is to publish and distribute inspirational products offering exceptional value and biblical encouragement to the masses.

Printed in the United States of America.
5 4 3 2 1

Acknowledgments

*T*ogether *E*veryone *A*ccomplishes *M*ore. My gratitude to the team that made this project a reality, including:

- Cathy, for your wise and wonderful wifely editing skills.
- My boys, Daniel, Andrew, and Luke, for liking all my books (or at least saying that you do).
- Carol and Sandy, my favorite sisters and PR persons.
- Susan Chittum, for your amazing ability to proofread what I write.
- The Mighty Men, for your prayers.
- Paul Muckley, for your passion for God and zeal to make this project a reality.
- Kelly Williams, for managing the in-house editorial process.
- Catherine Thompson, for handling the typesetting.
- Elmer Towns, Jamal Jivanjee, and the Arthur DeMoss family, for allowing me to tell your stories.

Contents

Introduction

Imagine that you have discovered a well-worn, leather-bound book. You slowly open it to find that it contains twenty-one checks. But unlike any other checkbook you have ever seen, each of these checks is already written. You become deeply puzzled when you read the "pay to the order of" line on the checks. Your name is already clearly written on each one.

Then your eyes fall on the "amount" section. Curious goose bumps burst out all over your arms when you see what is written there. The first one says, "Escape from Temptation"; the next, "Victory over Fear"; the check after that says, "Divine Guidance"; the next says, "A Blessed Life"; another reads, "Bad Turning into Good." You find that all twenty-one checks are made out to you. Each one offers an amazing blessing for your emotional and spiritual life.

"This must be a joke," you think. "This cannot be true." Slowly, fearfully, your eyes move down to the lower right-hand corner of the top check. Who signed these checks guaranteeing you so many promised blessings?

The signature line has one short word inscribed on it. You read this word and it staggers you. This is no joke. The payer's name is God.

I know what you are thinking. "Cute story, Dave. But I don't live in a fantasyland. Life is tough. Tell me something that will help me here and now in the real world."

I am about to tell you that very thing.

Today could be one of the most important days of your life. I say this because my story is not a joke. Figuratively speaking, God has given each of us an amazing checkbook written on the pages of the Bible. The book you are now reading highlights twenty-one amazing biblical checks and shows you the way to cash them.

How It All Began

It was an exciting but uncertain time in my life. Newly married, I was trying to clearly discern God's future plans for my wife and me. I needed provision, protection, and peace. Plus, I knew I needed more faith because I seemed to be easily swamped by fear.

At that time, as director of discipleship for Liberty University, I wrote a self-study Bible course entitled "Standing on the Promises." It was a simple survey of some of the 7,487 promises of God. I don't know how much this study helped the students, but it certainly encouraged me.

As I wrote that Bible study, I learned that each biblical promise tells us something of God and His love for His people. I found that His promises are faith-building guarantees from God Himself and that God is able to fulfill these promises.

It was thrilling to discover that God made promises that applied to all areas of my life and every event I encountered. Studying them brought me desperately needed inspiration, comfort, and challenge.

It's rather humbling, yet quite exciting, to realize that in some ways I'm back where I started when I was first married. I have gone full circle in my spiritual life and have returned to the place where I first stepped out in faith trusting the promises of God. The verses that were so precious to me twenty years ago are alive for me today in fresh, new ways. I am discovering how to be truly "rich" by trusting in the promises of God.

In this book I will share with you some of the most exciting, encouraging, and enriching promises in the Bible. As I do, I will dust off several colorful Bible characters who lived the promises. Their experiences will instruct, inspire, and meet your need as you cash each check in the checkbook of God's promises.

Many of the promises I will share with you are familiar. Most will be wonderfully comforting. All are extremely powerful.

As you study them, you will deepen your relationship with God as you intensify your faith and confidence in Him. These promises will breathe calm and peace into your hectic life. They have the power to lift you out of horizontal, temporal thinking into a vertical, eternal perspective of God's purposes. You will find your life enriched with renewed inner courage to bravely and boldly face the challenges of your life.

You Must Have Faith

I must confess, the concept of God's Word as a checkbook full of promises is not unique to me. About 130 years ago, a wise man named Charles H. Spurgeon wrote a little book called *Faith's Checkbook.* In it he said:

> *A promise from God may very instructively be compared to a check payable to order. It is given to the believer with the view of bestowing upon him some good thing. It is not meant that he should read it over comfortably, and then have done with it. No, he is to treat the promise as a reality, as a man treats a check. He is to take the promise and endorse it with his own name by personally receiving it as true. He is by faith to accept it as his own.*[1]

Wouldn't it be a tragedy if you left God's rich promises in the bank because you failed to believe that the checks we really made out to you? But such neglect occurs every

Everyone who owns a Bible has access to hundreds of promises. But these promises only encourage and enrich those who accept them by faith. For the rest, faith's checkbook lies unused and the owner unblessed.

You Must Cash the Checks

Years ago I read the account of a widow who, after her husband's death, barely had money to buy food and couldn't pay her bills. Her son, a successful businessman, heard reports of her stunning poverty and called her on the telephone:

"Mother, I hear that you don't have enough money to pay your bills."

"That's right," she said sadly.

"But how can that be? Don't you get my letters every month?"

"Yes, I get your letters," she sighed.

"Then what do you do with the money?" he asked. "I always send more than enough to cover all of your needs."

"What money?" she huffed. "All you ever send are those pretty slips of paper with your name scrawled on the bottom! I keep them in the desk drawer in case you might want them."

As it turned out, thousands of dollars of uncashed checks lay in her desk drawer. She lived in poverty even though she had more than enough money to meet all of her needs. If only she would have cashed those checks!

Before you are too hard on this poor widow, think about your situation. God has given you promises to cover your every … but they do you no good until you cash them.

…on's little book *Faith's Checkbook* tells us that once …ed a promise as our own by faith, we "must …e to the Lord, as a man presents a check at the counter of a bank. He must plead it by prayer, expecting to have it fulfilled."[2]

Believe me, God can pay up on anything He promised. He alone possesses unlimited strength, infinite power, and matchless wisdom! He can be trusted. It would be foolish and a great waste to possess a checkbook full of awesome blessings and not attempt to cash them because you don't believe that the check writer can pay.

Be Patient

Maybe you are reading this and thinking, "Yeah, that sounds good, but I claimed one of God's promises by faith in prayer once, and nothing happened."

I understand. But let's not forget the big picture.

There is only one true God in the universe—and it's not you. God is our heavenly Father who loves to bless His children. He is the guarantor of many amazing promises that only He can fulfill. But God is also the supremely wise and absolute ruler of the universe. This means that although He longs to bless you, He may not do it when or how you want. He is entitled to fulfill his promises exactly when and how He wants. Often He knows it is not best if we get what we want when we want it. Often it is best for us to wait. In His wisdom, God may choose that we do without small blessings now so He can pour out huge blessings later.

The Twenty-One Most Encouraging Promises of the Bible

Studying the promises of God can be like trying to drink out of a fire hydrant. They are so powerful and there are so many of them that they may knock us off our feet. We might come away wet but not refreshed. So I will focus on just twenty-one promises that share these characteristics:

1. *Most are conditional.* This means that before God will do His part, we have to do our part.

2. *All are evident in the life of a Bible character or characters.* Bible personalities bring God's promises to life.

3. *Each is especially encouraging.* Life can be hard and discouraging. These promises will breathe courage into your life and hope into your heart.

4. *All of the promises are universal.* They are as applicable in your twenty-first-century situation as when they were written.

Suggestions for Getting the Most Out of This Book

1. *Study each chapter with a prayerful heart.*
2. *Memorize the verse(s) containing the promise.*
3. *Share what you are learning with someone else.*
4. *Better still, study this book with a friend or a small group.*
5. *Reread chapters that especially apply to your needs.*
6. *Claim each promise in prayer.*
7. *Live what you learn.*

My Favorite Quotes about the Promises of God

Every promise of God is made for me.
MARTIN LUTHER

The future is as bright as the promises of God.
PIONEER MISSIONARY ADONIRAM JUDSON
(when asked about the prospects of taking the gospel to the nation of Burma)

A promise by God is a pledge by God. It provides the warrant and forms the basis of the prayer of faith.
J. O. SANDERS

God has always intended that His people should share His wealth and He has written a book to tell us so. The book contains the title deeds.
W. T. H. Richards

God's promises are never broken by leaning upon them.
Howard Hendricks

It is the prerogative of every believer to enter the inexhaustible mine of divine wealth, to search the sacred veins, to gather up the beautiful treasure that will enrich them. There is no excuse for spiritual poverty when we are invited to come and partake freely. Our inheritance is there to be taken and enjoyed.
W. T. H. Richards

Notes

1. Charles H. Spurgeon, *Faith's Checkbook* (Chicago: Moody Press, n.d.), ii.
2. Ibid., ii.

1

God's Promise of Escape from Temptation

1 CORINTHIANS 10:13

A deadly predator is out to get you. This marauder is cunning and shrewd. One moment its advance is subtle and apparently innocent. The next, it rises up and assaults with overwhelming force. This soul seducer can present itself as a harmless lamb, but it has the bite of a viper. It is both too beautiful to resist and too powerful to deny. This wicked shape-shifter will take any form necessary in order to persuade you to yield to its power.

You cannot let up, because your assailant won't. This relentless raider is always on the attack, never takes a break, never goes on vacation, and never takes a day off.

Be aware. Like a cagey boxer, this adversary will size you up quickly, diagnose your weaknesses, wait for an opening, or fake you into letting down your guard. Then, *bam!* It will drop you with an unexpected blow.

Temptation is a fierce foe—and it's after you. That's the bad news. The good news is that no matter how severe the temptation, you don't have to give in to it.

The Example of Joseph

If anyone ever had an excuse for giving in, it was Joseph. A powerful, "unattainable" woman, his master, Potiphar's wife, was freely offering herself to him. And Joseph was a healthy, red-blooded young man. And as they say, "Young men have needs." Surely, Joseph had his share of hormones. Besides that, he was far from home and had gone through a horrible ordeal. Certainly he was due a little pleasure. Plus, no one would know. And as his master's wife, this woman was Joseph's boss. How could he refuse her? On top of that, she had the power to significantly improve his life. Everything inside him said, "Go for it."

But Joseph firmly said, "No" (Genesis 39:7–9).

Unfortunately, the temptation didn't go away easily. Undaunted by his rebuff, Joseph's master's wife intensified her efforts to seduce him. Day after day, she made her appeal. Again and again, she enticed, she persuaded, she coaxed, she pleaded. Yet repeatedly Joseph resisted, refused, and rejected her advances (v. 10).

But just as he refused to give in, she stubbornly refused to give up.

One day her pride and lust would not go unfulfilled any longer. No one else was around. Desperately, she reached out for Joseph, grabbed his cloak, and pulled him down next to her. No man would resist such pressure.

But Joseph did. He jerked back so hard his cloak was left in her hands as he ran out of the room (vv. 11–15). This angered Potiphar's wife so severely she accused him of rape and had him thrown in prison (vv. 16–20). But the Lord was with Joseph and showed him His love (v. 21). So Joseph modeled faith in a promise that we can also claim.

You Are Not Alone in Temptation

> *No temptation has seized you except what is common to man. And God is faithful; he will not let you be tempted*

beyond what you can bear. But when you are tempted, he will also provide a way out so that you can stand up under it.

1 Corinthians 10:13

"No temptation has seized you except what is common to man." When we are tempted, we may think that we are the only one facing temptation. But that simply is not true. Humans have been facing temptation since the Garden of Eden. We all face it. Even Jesus faced temptation. It is part and parcel of the human condition.

Temptation is no respecter of persons. It pursues children and adults, men and women, the lost and the saved, the spiritually young and the spiritually mature. Pastors and missionaries face temptations as often as anyone else. When you battle temptation, you are not alone.

We also may assume that we are the only person who has ever faced a certain type or level of temptation. Again, this is not true. Every sin imaginable has existed as long as there have been people around to commit it. Certainly, you are a unique person. But you are not facing unique or special temptation.

A survey in *Discipleship Journal* ranked its readers' greatest spiritual challenges. They included the following:

1. Materialism
2. Pride
3. Self-centeredness
4. Laziness
5. Anger/bitterness tied with sexual lust
7. Envy
8. Gluttony
9. Lying[1]

I don't know about you, but I have wrestled with all of these and more. I could easily add selfish ambition, disobedience, doubt, distraction, rebellion, gossip, slander, worry, covetousness/greed, idolatry, and dishonesty to the list. I am sure there are many more that I have overlooked. The array of sins we are tempted to commit is more varied and numerous than the colors of the rainbow.

It's Not Irresistible

"God is faithful; he will not let you be tempted beyond what you can bear." This is the promise. No temptation is irresistible. Let me repeat that: No temptation is irresistible. God will not allow any temptation to be unbearable.

Note carefully that the basis for the ability to bear temptation is not our strength, wisdom, or willpower. Rather, it is God's faithfulness. Through this we can bear up under temptation just as Joseph did.

Note that the promise is not that we won't be tempted. We will. Count on it. Until we get to heaven, we will be tempted. It is a fact of life. Rather, the promise is that we won't face any temptation that is more than we can handle.

Let me clarify this. Temptation, in and of itself, is not sin. Temptation is the appeal to sin. It is possible to be tempted and not sin. The thought of sin is not sin until it is entertained and acted on. Alone in the wilderness, Jesus Himself, the holy Son of God, was tempted three times. Yet all three times He refused the temptation (Matthew 4:1–11). Likewise, God gives us the power to resist temptation. He who resisted temptation gives us victory over temptation.

The Great Escape

"But when you are tempted, he will also provide a way out so that you can stand up under it." A child of God has no excuse for sin. There is always a way to avoid it, because God is faithful to provide a way to avoid it or the power to resist it. That is His promise. But while it is God's responsibility to give us a way out, it is our responsibility to take the escape route.

Temptation came to Joseph several times in a variety of ways. Each time Potiphar's wife tried to seduce him, Joseph took an appropriate way of escape. Her first approach was a direct, surprise solicitation.

> *Now Joseph was well-built and handsome, and after a while his master's wife took notice of Joseph and said, "Come to bed with me!" But he refused. "With me in charge," he told her, "my master does not concern himself with anything in the house; everything he owns he has entrusted to my care. No one is greater in this house than I am. My master has withheld nothing from me except you, because you are his wife. How then could I do such a wicked thing and sin against God?"*
>
> GENESIS 39:6–9

Note that Joseph's first escape route was *firm refusal.* His strong sense of responsibility and accountability to his master and his steadfast reluctance to sin against God gave him the power to refuse and the way of escape.

Yet temptation is relentless. So Potiphar's lusty wife switched tactics to tempt Joseph by persistent appeal.

> *And though she spoke to Joseph day after day, he refused to go to bed with her or even be with her.*
>
> GENESIS 39:10

Joseph countered this constant insistence with *enduring denials.* But she would not take no for an answer.

> *One day he went into the house to attend to his duties, and none of the household servants was inside. She caught him by his cloak and said, "Come to bed with me!" But he left his cloak in her hand and ran out of the house.*
>
> GENESIS 39:11–12

When resistance and refusals are not enough, there is another way of escape, a literal one. *"Run for it."* That is exactly what Joseph did, leaving his jacket in her clutching fingers.

God is faithful to help us avoid temptation and can be quite creative in helping us run from it.

God Has a Sense of Humor

During my last year in high school, I dated a very attractive young lady. One warm evening we were driving around and pulled off the side of the road to talk in a secluded section of a quiet neighborhood. As a newly committed Christian, I was convicted about maintaining a high level of purity in my relationships with girls. Yet I had foolishly put myself in a place of temptation. When there was a pause in the conversation, she scooted over on the bench seat, began to stroke the hair on the back of my head, and smiled knowingly.

I don't need to tell you that my hormones were hopping out of my skin. Silently, I shot a prayer up to God: "Lord, please get me out of this before we do something we'll later regret."

She began to lean in closer. I gulped as my heart began to pound. Then her eyes got as big as saucers, and she pointed over my shoulder as she screamed, "What is that?"

I turned my head and found myself eyeball-to-eyeball with a huge dog. I jerked back, scared that the monster dog would bite my face off. But the gentle giant was content to just look at us.

"Shoo!" I said hoarsely, trying to sound brave. Colossus the Canine just blinked happily. We looked out of the windows and found that a posse of seven or eight dogs of all shapes, sizes, and colors surrounded us. There were little fat ones and medium-sized, sleek ones. Most were well groomed, but some were scruffy mutts.

"Get!" I said even more loudly. Then, mustering as much authority as I could, I said, "Get outta here!"

With that, the enormous beast pulled his head out of the car window and began to lumber off. His motley crew of mutts followed in a happy pack, looking for mischief. My date and I just laughed. "I guess it's time to get you home," I said, relieved that I had been rescued by a bunch of neighborhood dogs out for a night on the town.

Who would have believed it? What were the odds of a Great Dane being loose in that neighborhood at that time? It was a chance in a million that he would stick his big head into an open car window at exactly the moment a weak child of God desperately needed a way of escape. What can I say except God uses whatever means are at hand in order to keep His promises.

A Final Encouragement

You do not have to be defeated by temptation. You can win by taking the way of escape. God will be faithful to provide one. Joseph used several escape routes, and so can you.

Note

1. Stanley J. Grenz, "Don't Take the Bait! The Best Time to Fight Temptation Is Before It Strikes," Discipleship Journal, November/December, 1992, http://www.navpress.com/EPubs/DisplayArticle/1/1.72.3.html.

God's Promise of Victory over Fe

Isaiah 43:1–2

I used to be fearless, with the emphasis on *used to* few untimely setbacks occurred and some huge obstacl a major dose of reality knocked the edge off my overconfi I imagine you might be the same. Adversaries loom large the horizon. Potential defeat hangs in the air like a dark clou Uncertainty about the unknown makes it tough to stride boldly into the fog of the future.

Fear can be an unwelcome companion and a paralyzing partner. It zaps our strength, runs off with our joy, murders our peace, and stomps the spring out of our step. Yet God promises that no matter how hot the fire or how high the flood, we can face it without fear.

A *Fearful Fire*

Heat resonated off the giant furnace so intensely it created visual ripples in the air. Huge slippery drops of sweat rolled off the guards as they pushed the three tightly bound young men up the stairs to the awful agony of the excruciating execution. Massive, menacing flames danced merrily up to the sky. Billows of smoke swirled above the furnace in a hungry, wicked grin. All other noise was sucked out of the stifling air by the roaring bellow of the ravenous blaze.

Shadrach, Meshach, and Abednego were going to die and

Soon smoke would pour into their lungs and choke ıercilessly. The heat of the fire would char their skin ›efore melting the flesh from their bones—all because ‹ould not worship the king of Babylon.

Idolatrous King

ıg Nebuchadnezzar was the most powerful man in the greatt nation on earth. His capital, Babylon, was unrivaled in ‹ealth and beauty. "In addition to its size," wrote Herodotus, a historian in 450 BC, "Babylon surpasses in splendor any city in the known world."[1] Rising above the city was the famous temple to the god Marduk that seemed to reach to the heavens.

During his long reign, King Nebuchadnezzar had constructed an astonishing array of temples, streets, palaces, walls, and gardens. His mountainous terraced trophies, the Hanging Gardens, were so stunning in beauty and amazing in architecture that they have been acclaimed as one of the Seven Wonders of the Ancient World.

When Nebuchadnezzar decided that he had achieved the lofty status of god, he had a giant gold statue made in his likeness. It stood ninety feet high and proudly proclaimed the glory of the king. Nebuchadnezzar ordered all of the important officials in his kingdom to come and bow before his image—or die. Included in this order were three young Hebrew men. They had been taken captive from Jerusalem, raised in the culture of the Babylonians, and given positions in the king's cabinet. With the privilege came the responsibility of unquestioned obedience to the mighty rule of Nebuchadnezzar.

Jealous conspirators used the king's order as an opportunity to corner and accuse these three Jews. Gleefully, they told the king of Shadrach, Meshach, and Abednego's failure to bow and worship at the feet of the golden statue. This infuriated the king, so he ordered them to be brought before him.

Normal men quivered in the presence of this most powerful man on earth. Many were those who suffered torture and death for making him upset. The three young men had good reason to fear.

But they didn't.

Three Courageous Believers

The king threatened to kill them. But Shadrach, Meshach, and Abednego were fearless and resolute.

> *Shadrach, Meshach and Abednego replied to the king, "O Nebuchadnezzar, we do not need to defend ourselves before you in this matter. If we are thrown into the blazing furnace, the God we serve is able to save us from it, and he will rescue us from your hand, O king. But even if he does not, we want you to know, O king, that we will not serve your gods or worship the image of gold you have set up."*
>
> Daniel 3:16–18

What confidence! "God is able to save us. He will rescue us."

What courage! "Even if He does not, we will not serve your gods or worship your image."

What insanity! Nebuchadnezzar was no one to tease or trifle with. They had better be ready to back up their boldness with commitment.

Obviously, Nebuchadnezzar did not want to hear such bold declarations. Incensed, he ordered the execution furnace heated to seven times its normal temperature. It was so incredibly hot that the guards who dropped them into it died carrying out their orders. The three Hebrews would catch fire like dry kindling and be consumed in minutes.

A Fourth Man in the Fire

Eagerly, Nebuchadnezzar peered into the furnace. He was not expecting what he saw. Shocked and stunned, he turned to his advisers and asked,

> *"Weren't there three men that we tied up and threw into the fire?" They replied, "Certainly, O king." He said, "Look! I see four men walking around in the fire, unbound and unharmed, and the fourth looks like a son of the gods."*
>
> DANIEL 3:24–25

He got it all right except the last part. Yes, Shadrach, Meshach, and Abednego were all alive. Yes, they were now unbound. Yes, they were unharmed. Yes, there was a fourth figure in the fire, but the fourth was not merely "*like* a son of the gods." He *was* the Son of God!

Jesus went through the fire with Shadrach, Meshach, and Abednego. And He'll do the same for you.

Shadrach, Meshach, and Abednego not only walked out unharmed, but they did not even smell of smoke (Daniel 3:27)! Nebuchadnezzar was impressed.

> *Then Nebuchadnezzar said, "Praise be to the God of Shadrach, Meshach and Abednego, who has sent his angel and rescued his servants! They trusted in him and defied the king's command and were willing to give up their lives rather than serve or worship any god except their own God. Therefore I decree that the people of any nation or language who say anything against the God of Shadrach, Meshach and Abednego be cut into pieces and their houses be turned into piles of rubble, for no other god can save*

> *in this way." Then the king promoted Shadrach, Meshach and Abednego in the province of Babylon.*
>
> DANIEL 3:28–30

What an awesome story of divine protection and human courage! They lived through the fire. They were so completely unharmed by it, they did not even smell of smoke. Their testimony was told throughout the nation. And they got a promotion! All this happened because Shadrach, Meshach, and Abednego had the courage to face their fire with the Lord.

We must ask several questions. Where did they get such courage? How could they face execution unafraid? Is it possible for us to be as fearless and bold as they?

The answers are found in a promise.

A Faithful Promise

Prior to the Babylonian captivity, Isaiah, a Hebrew prophet, ministered in Jerusalem. Isaiah recorded a promise that sounds eerily applicable to their situation.

> *But now, this is what the* LORD *says—he who created you, O Jacob, he who formed you, O Israel: "Fear not, for I have redeemed you; I have summoned you by name; you are mine. When you pass through the waters, I will be with you; and when you pass through the rivers, they will not sweep over you. When you walk through the fire, you will not be burned; the flames will not set you ablaze.*
>
> ISAIAH 43:1–2

Notice the last sentence: "When you walk through the fire, you will not be burned; the flames will not set you ablaze."

Not only were they unburned; they did not even smell of smoke.

We all face fires in our lives. By "fires" I mean those dangerous, painful, terrifying situations and seasons when it seems there is no possible way to survive. Maybe it's a divorce, a very sick child, the death of a loved one, a lost job, a lawsuit, or a health issue. A fire can be anything that threatens to consume us.

Perhaps Isaiah's image of a flood is more appropriate for your situation. Like a flood, the pressure in your life builds higher and higher. It threatens to wash away everything you love or carry you away. It feels overwhelming.

Whether fires or floods, the Lord promises not to protect us *from* them but to protect us *in* them. We need not fear.

Fear Not, God Is with You in the Fire

Reading Isaiah's promise, I find special comfort in the phrase, "I will be with you." It is important to know that Jesus did not keep Shadrach, Meshach, and Abegnego from going into the fire. They were thrown into it. But when they went into the fire, He went through it with them. They were not alone. And neither are you alone in your personal fires and floods.

Certainly, fires and floods have a way of making us feel isolated. The terrifying nature of out-of-control events leaves us feeling afraid and very alone. But God is there with us. This is His promise.

Fear Not, God Will Help You

The encouragement to "fear not" and the promise of God's presence in fearful events are reiterated elsewhere by Isaiah:

> *Do not fear, for I am with you; do not be dismayed, for I am your God. I will strengthen you and help you; I will uphold you with my righteous right hand.*
>
> Isaiah 41:10

Here God does not merely promise to be with us but goes further by guaranteeing to help us. When the flames blaze or the floodwaters swirl, we definitely need His help. And He will help us.

Fear Not, I Will Hold You by the Hand

When the flames are crackling hungrily or the floodwaters are swirling crazily, it is easy to lose your sense of direction. Confusion reigns, compounding fear. This is when you need someone to hold your hand and walk you through the danger. Even better, the divine Someone will take you by the hand and guide you.

> *For I am the Lord, your God, who takes hold of your right hand and says to you, Do not fear; I will help you.*
>
> Isaiah 41:13

Twenty-First-Century Supernatural Courage

She had lived in her apartment only two days. She got out of the car and walked to the door. Ashley Smith felt fear well up inside as a man came up out of the shadows behind her, stuck a gun to her head, and forced her inside.

The fear spread more deeply when she realized that she was the hostage of accused rapist and murderer Brian Nichols. Hours earlier, Nichols had escaped from an Atlanta courthouse, leaving a trail of blood and four dead in his wake. He just happened to show up at her door.

Smith, a twenty-six-year-old widow, was newly involved in a Celebrate Recovery group at a local church. There she sought help to overcome her battle with drug and alcohol addiction. Fearing rape and murder, Smith looked to God for courage.

As the night passed, she slowly won Nichols's confidence. Eventually she told him he needed to turn himself in and stop hurting people. She said that he needed to go to prison and share the Word of God with the prisoners.

The next morning, as Ashley Smith calmly served him pancakes, the murderer-rapist Brian Nichols looked at her and said that he believed she was an angel sent from God. He was lost and needed her to tell him to stop hurting people. Eventually he allowed her to leave. Shortly after, he surrendered to the police.

Newspapers across America reported that God gave Ashley Smith supernatural courage to overcome her fear in order to minister in an abnormally dangerous and unusual situation. She said, "I believe God brought him to my door so he would not hurt anyone else."[2]

A *Final Encouragement*

God can give you all you need to overcome your fear. If God can do it for Shadrach, Meshach, Abednego, and Ashley Smith, He can do it for you. That is His promise. Trust Him.

Notes

1. "The Hanging Gardens of Babylon," http://www.unmuseum.org/hangg.htm (June 13, 2005).

2. "I Felt Really, Really Scared," CNN, March 15, 2005, http://www.cnn.com/2005/LAW/03/14/atlanta.hostage.

3

God's Promise of Divine Guidance

PROVERBS 3:5–6

Decisions—life is full of decisions. This reality starts to hit home near the end of high school when everyone begins to ask what you are planning to do after graduation. Unfortunately, if you answer, "Go to college," that just brings more questions. What college? What are you going to major in? And how are you going to pay for it?

A few years out of high school, the interrogations shift to career and marriage decisions. Then the questions revolve around having children and educating them. As we move along through life, we face constant career choices, housing options, church alternatives, ministry opportunities, and more. How do we decide?

Who you are today is the product of the decisions you have made in the past. Who you become tomorrow will be the result of the decisions you make today. How do you know whether you are making the right decisions? What do you do when you need direction? Fortunately, God's Word gives simple, clear, encouraging directions. It is all found in one of the most encouraging promises in the Bible:

> *Trust in the LORD with all your heart, and lean not on your own understanding; in all your ways acknowledge Him, and He shall direct your paths.*
>
> PROVERBS 3:5–6 NKJV

And He Shall Direct Your Paths

I love the last six words of this promise. They clearly and confidently proclaim that God will do His part. He *will* direct your paths, make your next step clear, and keep you on track. What a relief! It is possible to be in step with God, follow His plan, make the right decision, and know the next step. We do not have to fear that we will make a bad decision, miss what God has for us, and end up ruining our life.

When we feel overwhelmed by decisions, it is encouraging to know that God will do His part. But we have to do ours.

> *Trust in the LORD with all your heart, and lean not on your own understanding; in all your ways acknowledge Him.*

God's promise of direction is contingent upon our relationship with Him. We need to trust in, depend upon, and confide in Him from the bottom of our hearts. We can't go halfway. We must go the distance in relying on Him and not ourselves.

I am a big believer in getting good information and informed advice. When facing major decisions, I usually make a chart of pros and cons. But trusting in the Lord must supersede this. It must come ahead of our own understanding. Once we have gathered all the facts, sorted through all the advice, and examined our own hearts, we need to give it all over to God and follow Him, no matter what.

When we trust the Lord, He may lead us in paths that don't make much sense from a human perspective. We can't always figure it all out on our own. Remember, He is God and we are not. He can see further and more clearly into the future than we can. We may not accurately discern the next step, but He can see the whole path and process. We may not see upcoming potholes and land mines. We do not even fully understand our own deepest desires, but He does.

According to the promise, our responsibility in securing divine guidance includes knowing, recognizing, and acknowledging Him in all our ways. The Lord must be our focal point in the decision-making process. We must keep our ears open to His voice as we surrender our plans, priorities, dreams, and desires to Him. We must trust Him even if it doesn't immediately make sense to do so.

Trusting When It Doesn't Make Sense

My mentor, Dr. Elmer Towns, has had a long and fruitful career as a Christian leader and author. One day he had to trust God for direction when doing so didn't make sense. He had resigned his job as a teacher at a small Bible college in order to take a more prestigious job traveling and speaking to diverse denominations and at various conventions. In his mind, this was the perfect job—travel, influence, ministry to many churches, and national recognition. He saw it as a golden opportunity, but God had a different plan.

Dr. Towns wrote about his experience later:

> *I woke up violently in the middle of a black night. Something was wrong. I began to sweat all over.*
>
> *"Lord, what is it?"*
>
> *The Lord was in the room, not physically, nor did I see a vision, nor did I hear an audible voice; but I knew that the Lord was standing by my bed to warn me of something.... I prayed several times, "Lord, what are you trying to tell me?"*
>
> *Then the Lord spoke to my heart, telling me not to*

take the new job I had just accepted.... "Don't take the job," God kept saying.

As I wrestled with God, I reviewed my long-range priorities. I asked myself what those priorities were. I also considered my strongest gifts, and how I could make the greatest contribution with my life. I confessed to the Lord that I was ego driven. Ever since I was a freshman in Bible college, I wanted to be a Bible-college president. I had rationalized that the fame I would get from the new position of traveling for Sunday School would open up a door into a Bible college somewhere, sometime. But every time I talked to God, I got the same message: "Don't take the Sunday School job."

After a couple of hours of praying, I surrendered before the Lord. I told Him that fame was not important. I surrendered my reputation and even said, "God, if I never become a Bible-college president, Thy will be done!"[1]

By faith Elmer put God's will above his own even though it did not make sense. As he did this, he said that he felt God saying, "Don't take the Sunday school job. . .but within a year I will give you a college presidency." Elmer resigned the new prestigious position and continued teaching at the small Bible college. He also continued to trust in the Lord with all his heart and acknowledge His voice. And God did not forget His promise.

Six months later Elmer decided to drive home the long way, past his church. Seeing his pastor's car, he stopped and went in to chat. Soon into the conversation, he blurted out his heart's desire. "Someday, I want to be a Bible-college president."

While his pastor confirmed this dream as valid, based on

Elmer Towns's drive and abilities, the phone rang. On the other end was a friend of the pastor. Oddly, the man asked, "Do you know where we can find a young man to be president of Winnipeg Bible College?"

The pastor grinned at Towns and said, "Your man is sitting right here."[2]

Later Towns wrote:

> *I could hear the voice of God whispering in my other ear, "See. . .I told you that if you wouldn't take the Sunday school job, I'd have a college presidency for you within a year."*[3]

What had happened? Elmer Towns, a young Bible-college professor, had faced a decision. He made what he thought was a good decision to take a prestigious job traveling and speaking. God said, "No." Elmer surrendered his dreams to God, trusting God from the bottom of his heart. He obeyed God's voice even when it did not make sense. The Lord directed his paths and gave him the desire of his heart.

The Desires of Your Heart

> *Delight yourself also in the LORD, and He shall give you the desires of your heart. Commit your way to the LORD, trust also in Him, and He shall bring it to pass.*
>
> PSALM 37:4–5 NKJV

I believe that God gives us the desires of our hearts in a two-fold fashion. First, He writes them into our hearts—sometimes so deeply that we don't fully realize them. He gives us a burden, a passion, a vision of some good thing that we want to see occur in our lives in the future. He later makes them become a reality.

Long before Elmer's experience, God had etched into his heart the deep desire to be a Bible-college president. When the timing was right, God made it a reality. Between the promise and the fulfillment, Elmer did his part. He delighted himself in the Lord and committed his way to Him. He made the Lord his highest desire. He surrendered his future into God's hands, even when it did not make sense. And then God put all the pieces together to make it a wonderful reality. It all worked out according to God's plan for Elmer's future.

A Future and a Hope

> *"I know the plans I have for you," declares the* LORD*, "plans to prosper you and not to harm you, plans to give you hope and a future. Then you will call upon me and come and pray to me, and I will listen to you. You will seek me and find me when you seek me with all your heart."*
>
> JEREMIAH 29:11–13

It is encouraging to know that God does not forget or abandon us. He has plans for us. His plans are positive and even include true prosperity. He promises to take care of us and not abandon us. He gives us hope and a future.

But in order to experience God's plans, we must call on Him and seek Him with all of our hearts. He must be the priority of our thoughts and the object of our trust. We need to make the Lord the focal point of our decision-making process.

A *Final Encouragement*

I do not know what decisions you are facing today, but the Lord does. He has not forgotten you. Your future is important to Him; He just wants to be trusted. He desires that you seek Him and His will above all else. He may not wake you up in the middle of the night, but if you really trust him, He will direct your path.

NOTES

1. Elmer Towns, *God Encounters* (Ventura, CA: Regal Books), 2000, 16. Used by permission.
2. Ibid., 17.
3. Ibid., 18.

4

God's Promise of a Blessed Life

PSALM 1:1–3

What if you were promised true happiness? What if someone guaranteed you a stable life? What if they gave you the assurance of a productive, fruitful life and pledged that you would become strong and resilient through the dry seasons? What if they even promised prosperity on top of all the rest?

Would you believe it?

You should, because Someone has made such a promise and can deliver on it. But before we get to the promise, let me first tell you about a man who experienced it. His name was Ezra.

The Story of a Blessed Life

Ezra was a Jewish man living in Persia nearly five hundred years before the birth of Jesus. The Jews were in Persia because the Babylonian army had taken them captive years earlier and brought them to Babylon as slaves.

Ezra's heritage was that of a Hebrew priest. His job was to serve in the royal archives of the Persian Empire. As a scribe, he had access to the Word of God. Eventually his Bible study fanned into flame a burden for his people and a desire to return to Jerusalem.

Because Ezra's heart was aligned with God's Word and his passion linked with God's heart, God poured His blessing out on Ezra. Amazingly, when Ezra asked the pagan king to allow him to take a contingent of Jews back to Jerusalem, the king agreed. When Ezra asked the king to pay the bill for this journey, the king said yes. Even when Ezra asked to rebuild the Jewish temple and restore the Jewish community, the king supported him.

So Ezra led his band of pilgrims on the long and perilous five-month journey back to Jerusalem. In spite of the great odds against them, they arrived in Jerusalem safe and sound. There, Ezra succeeded in his massive undertakings to restore the community and rebuild the temple. He also helped Nehemiah rebuild the walls around the city. On top of that, he led the people in a time of revived obedience and renewed relationships with God. And if that was not enough, he wrote several books of the Bible.

The Jewish nation could have easily been assimilated into the pagan Persian culture if Ezra had not come on the scene. He gave his people back their city, their temple, their religion, and their distinctiveness. Humanly speaking, Jerusalem would have remained in shambles without the incredibly successful and visionary efforts of Ezra. He was a man who prospered on every level. By all accounts, he lived a blessed life.

One phrase repeatedly appears in the autobiographic story of Ezra's life. "The hand of the LORD my God was on me" (Ezra 7:6, 28; 8:18, 22, 31). Ezra knew that God richly blessed everything he did. He also knew why.

The Secret of a Blessed Life

While Ezra was writing the official records of the Jewish people, he revealed the secret of his success. Sometimes Ezra wrote about himself in the third person. Note carefully what he said.

The gracious hand of his God was on him. For Ezra had devoted himself to the study and observance of the Law of the LORD, and to teaching its decrees and laws in Israel.

EZRA 7:9–10

God blessed Ezra's life so richly because Ezra based his life so completely on God's Word. The secret of Ezra's success was the fact that he lived a Scripture-centered life.

Prior to returning to Jerusalem, restoring the Jewish community, and rebuilding the Jewish temple, Ezra had access to the Word of God. He had an opportunity few others enjoyed at that time; he could personally examine the Hebrew law and the records of the Hebrew kings. Ezra had access to all of the Word of God that had been written by that time. He did not take this privilege lightly. He devoted himself to the lifelong habit of studying, living, and teaching the Word of God.

Others had the same access to God's Word as Ezra enjoyed, but their names are long forgotten by history. Ezra did not just have access to the Word of God; he committed himself to it. He put his whole heart into it. It shaped him, including his values, decisions, attitudes, and actions. He invested his time, energy, and effort into studying, living, and teaching the Word of God. It was the secret of his success.

A Man Who Knew the Secret of Blessing

I had the privilege of attending college with Mark DeMoss. One day in chapel, Mark's father, Arthur DeMoss, was the guest speaker. Art and his wife, Nancy, were known for hosting evangelistic dinner parties to reach executives with the gospel of Jesus. A devoted Christian father and highly successful businessman, Art had founded a large insurance company.

He passed away a few years later, but his influence remains. The Arthur S. DeMoss Foundation supports evangelism through the *Power for Living* television commercials and book distributions. The foundation is also one of the largest philanthropic organizations in the country. DeMoss led a thriving Christian family that continues to make an impact for Christ. By any measure, Art DeMoss was a blessed, prosperous successful man.

This plain, lively, straightforward Greek gentleman full of common sense and biblical advice immediately connected with the audience of students that day in chapel. During his talk, Art gave the threefold secret of his success, and I have never forgotten what he said. He told how, as a struggling young businessman, he discovered God's secret of success. His secret was his commitment to give God the first hour of every day, the first day of every week, and the first dime of every dollar. Soon he was out of debt and his business took off. More important, his family flourished and his ministry to executives was launched.

A decade later, Nancy Leigh DeMoss, Art's daughter and a best-selling Christian author in her own right, had this to say about her dad:

> *As I look back on my dad's life, I see several reasons for the blessing of God on his life. First, He put God first above everything else. He believed that the greatest wealth was in knowing God. This priority was evident as he gave the first hour of every day to the study of God's Word and prayer. In the twenty-eight years that he knew Christ, there was not a single day when anything else came before that hour alone with God. He put God first in his business, in spite of the prevailing opinion that biblical ethics cannot be applied in the business world. God proved that His way works!*[1]

Art DeMoss was incredibly blessed because he gave God the first hour of every day by studying God's Word and praying. He then spent the rest of the day trying to live and share what he had learned in the morning. Just like Ezra, he lived a life devoted to the Word of God, studying, living, and teaching it. And God blessed him for it.

Ezra's Secret of a Blessed Life

It is likely that Ezra collected the Psalms as we know them today. Of all 150 psalms, Ezra chose one in particular to lead the collection. It is foundational to the rest. I also believe that it was his personal favorite, because he obviously patterned his life after it. It contains God's promise of prosperity.

> *Blessed is the man who does not walk in the counsel of the wicked or stand in the way of sinners or sit in the seat of mockers. But his delight is in the law of the* LORD, *and on his law he meditates day and night. He is like a tree planted by streams of water, which yields its fruit in season and whose leaf does not wither. Whatever he does prospers.*
>
> PSALM 1:1–3

Computer geeks used to talk about GIGO. GIGO stands for garbage in, garbage out. Input is everything. A computer is a neutral tool. It does not create good or bad; it only spits out what has been entered.

In many ways, our minds are like computers. Input is everything. Our minds cannot produce good thoughts, feelings, or actions if they have not received good data. Psalm 1 promises blessing on the one who deliberately decides to monitor the data entering his or her mind. Here are ways to do this:

- *Limit Negative Input*

Blessed is the man who does not walk in the counsel of the wicked or stand in the way of sinners or sit in the seat of mockers.

Psalm 1:1

How well God must like you—you don't hang out at Sin Saloon, you don't slink along Dead-End Road, you don't go to Smart-Mouth College.

Psalm 1:1 The Message

Blessed (happy, fortunate, prosperous, and enviable) is the man who walks and lives not in the counsel of the ungodly [following their advice, their plans and purposes], nor stands [submissive and inactive] in the path where sinners walk, nor sits down [to relax and rest] where the scornful [and the mockers] gather.

Psalm 1:1 Amplified

The word "blessed" describes a life of rich happiness and deep satisfaction. This blessed life begins when we accept responsibility to monitor what goes into our minds. We need to be keenly aware of the amount of negative, ungodly, or even neutral data we take in. We must carefully consider the people we spend time with, the music we listen to, the movies and television shows we watch, the books and magazine we read, and the Web sites we visit. The secret of the blessed life begins by restricting the amount of nonbiblical information we receive.

- *Love Positive Input*

But his delight is in the law of the LORD, and on his law he meditates day and night.

PSALM 1:2

Instead you thrill to GOD'S Word, you chew on Scripture day and night.

PSALM 1:2 THE MESSAGE

But his delight and desire are in the law of the Lord, and on His law (the precepts, the instructions, the teachings of God) he habitually meditates (ponders and studies) by day and by night.

PSALM 1:2 AMPLIFIED

The blessed life is built on the choice to fill our thoughts with the truth of God's Word. As God's Word saturates our minds, it will enhance our attitudes and guide our actions. The result will be the kind of life that God cannot help but bless.

Notice that the ones who are blessed not only delight in the Word; they act on their desire. They meditate on Scripture. They think it over, ponder its meaning, pray it out, study it more deeply, recall it often, and consider how to apply it. God's Word is the controlling lens by which everything else is viewed, the standard by which everything else is judged, the foundation on which everything else is added, and the compass by which every decision is made.

Blessed Prosperity

> *He is like a tree planted by streams of water, which yields its fruit in season and whose leaf does not wither. Whatever he does prospers.*
>
> Psalm 1:3

When a person truly lives a Scripture-centered life, he or she is like a tree planted by rivers of water—vital, stable, fruitful, durable, and successful.

A *Final* Encouragement

Ezra, Art DeMoss, and many others found that the secret to a blessed life is daily dedication to the Word of God. God's promise will work for you if you, too, will make a serious commitment to the Word of God.

Note

1. Taken from *A Legacy of Giving: Lessons from the Life of a Father* by Nancy Leigh DeMoss, © 2003. Used by permission of Revive Our Hearts, www.reviveourhearts.com.

5

God's Promise of Bad Turning into Good

ROMANS 8:28

"I went to sleep with gum in my mouth and now there's gum in my hair and when I got out of bed this morning I tripped on the skateboard and by mistake I dropped my sweater in the sink while the water was running and I could tell it was going to be a terrible, horrible, no good, very bad day."

So begin the trials and tribulations of the irascible Alexander, as told by Judith Viorst in her book *Alexander and the Terrible, Horrible, No Good, Very Bad Day.* As poor Alexander's day progresses, he faces a barrage of bummers worthy of a bad country-and-western song. Alexander offers us a cranky retelling of that awful day of seemingly endless mishaps and misfortunes, including getting crushed in the middle seat of the car, a lunch sack with no dessert, a cavity at the dentist's office, sneakers with no stripes, lima beans for supper, nothing but kissing on television, being forced to sleep in the dreaded railroad-train pajamas, and the final indignity of being rejected by the cat that wants to sleep with his brother, Anthony, not with him. Alexander's conclusion is that it would be best to move to Australia.

The reason this book has remained a popular classic with children and adults for over thirty years is because we all have days like Alexander's, and we can't buy a break. Too often, such terrible, horrible, no good, very bad days pile up into awful, horrendous, rotten weeks. Too many of those dreadful weeks can leave us buried under an avalanche of discouragement and despair.

Bad things happen to all of us, even when we are trying to be good. Sometimes when we are living our best, we experience the worst. That's bad news. But the good news is that God is big enough to turn every tad of bad into good.

Unlike Alexander, we have a better option than moving to Australia. We have a wonderful book called the Bible filled with promises that inject high-octane encouragement into our deflated souls. Joseph experienced one of these promises. His life makes Alexander's terrible, horrible, no good, very bad day look like a picnic in paradise.

A Dream Turns into a Nightmare

Upside down. Suddenly, violently, unexpectedly, awfully, Joseph's life turned upside down. God reached down and, in one ugly event, jerked him out of his comfortable existence filled with bright potential and stuffed him into a coffin of slavery. Here's what happened:

Seventeen-year old Joseph awoke one morning both excited and scared. God had given him a dream of becoming a leader. He had been given a glimpse of his destiny. Yet in his excitement and enthusiasm while sharing his dream, Joseph unwittingly offended his jealous older brothers. This was not good.

Soon, events turned ugly. Joseph was doing what his father had asked as he went to get a report on how his brothers were getting along grazing the family flocks. Little did Joseph suspect that their jealousy would lead them to kidnap him, throw him into an empty well, and sell him to slave traders headed for Egypt (see Genesis 37:1–28).

That is how his dream turned into a nightmare. It must have felt like a punch to the gut when Joseph, formerly the favorite son of a wealthy shepherd, woke to find himself a slave in Egypt.

But slowly his life got better—temporarily better, that is. Joseph's hard work and skill as a leader eventually elevated his status until he was put in charge of managing the household of Potiphar, Pharaoh's captain of the guard. Things were looking up when it all came crashing down.

A *Slave Becomes a Convict*

As I mentioned earlier, Potiphar's lonely wife made a series of unsuccessful passes at Joseph. Yet Joseph loved God and felt too much responsibility to his master to give in to her temptations. She was embarrassed and angry that he refused her advances, so she accused him of rape. The next thing he knew, Joseph was in prison and life looked uglier. Yet it got worse (see Genesis 39:1–20).

At first, his situation in prison contained a thread of promise. Joseph was again given an opportunity to develop as a leader. He also got to associate with some very intelligent and formerly high-ranking political prisoners (39:21–40:4). While in prison, Joseph had the unusual opportunity of predicting that the king's cupbearer would be restored to his former position. When he made this prediction, Joseph hoped that the cupbearer would air his unjust plight and plead his case to Pharaoh.

But when the cupbearer was restored to his position, he forgot Joseph (40:5–23).

Years went by.

Rejected by his family, sold into slavery, cast into prison, and now forgotten and left to rot behind bars, Joseph had one bad experience after another. But God promises to work all things—even very bad things—for the good of those who love Him and are called according to His purpose. That's just what happened to Joseph.

From Prisoner to Prime Minister

Two years after the cupbearer resumed his post, Pharaoh awoke in a cold sweat from a night of unusual dreams. None of his advisers could interpret these dreams. Eventually the cupbearer remembered Joseph and told Pharaoh about him. Pharaoh called for the prisoner, told him the dream, and waited. Skillfully, Joseph interpreted the dream and laid out a plan for dealing with its implications. Pharaoh was so impressed that he made Joseph the prime minister of the entire nation. From his position, Joseph prepared for the coming famine and saved the lives of many people, including his own family (41:1–57).

Joseph had traveled down a deep, difficult, and lonely road of kidnapping, slavery, and prison. Yet the boy with a dream of leading his family now led the number one nation in the world! God had taken all of the bad events in Joseph's life and skillfully put them together like pieces in a puzzle to create a beautiful picture. Consider the following:

- Joseph learned more about leadership in Potiphar's house and as a prisoner than he would have learned in the comfort of his father's home. God had worked much that was bad to produce a greater good.
- Because he was in prison, Joseph met some royal officials and was thus strategically placed to be able to explain Pharaoh's dream. God again took something bad and used it to accomplish good.

- Because this all happened in Egypt, Joseph was able to serve in the most influential nation on earth. Yet again God turned much bad into more good.

None of the good things in Joseph's life could have happened without the bad. Like a skilled weaver, God used ugly events, evil people, unjust treatment, and long imprisonment to weave a beautiful tapestry. Like an elite chef, He cooked up a delicious stew out of the leftovers languishing in the pantry of Joseph's life. God turned horrendous bad into great good.

God Turns Harm into Good

Several years later Joseph confronted his guilty brothers. Most men in his position would have had them imprisoned or killed. They were deathly afraid of him, with good reason. But fortunately for them, Joseph saw the bigger picture and understood the ways of God.

> *His brothers then came and threw themselves down before him. "We are your slaves," they said. But Joseph said to them, "Don't be afraid. Am I in the place of God? You intended to harm me, but God intended it for good to accomplish what is now being done, the saving of many lives."*
>
> GENESIS 50:18–20

Joseph was not bitter toward his brothers, because he saw that what they intended for bad God worked out for good for him, for them, and for the whole world. Multiplied good came out of misguided bad. Joseph was living the promise of Romans 8:28 two thousand years before it was written!

Bad into Good

And we know that in all things God works for the good of those who love him, who have been called according to his purpose.

ROMANS 8:28

This verse imparts confidence to us when things appear to be utterly awful. It tells us of the comprehensive power of God to work every detail in our lives, even the ugly ones, into something beautiful. It also encourages each of us to build a deep love life with God. After all, He has given us this promise.

We Need to Love Him

This promise is unbounded as to what God can use for good. But it is limited as to whom He'll bless in this way. His responsibility is to change trials into triumphs. Our responsibility is to be people who qualify for this promise. The promise of changing bad things into good is given only to those who love God.

Whole books have been written on what it means to love God. This is not the focus of this book. Remember, however, that when trouble comes, it is a reminder to reexamine your love relationship with God. It helps to realign our priorities, motives, and attitudes.

Advancing the Gospel

The apostle Paul recorded the promise of Romans 8:28. He certainly loved God. He also had plenty of bad experiences in his life. On one occasion, he and his missionary partner, Silas, were evangelizing the city of Philippi. After they set free a demon-possessed girl, authorities had Paul and Silas thrown in jail. The enemy certainly meant this for evil. But God used it for good. Through a divinely sanctioned earthquake, Paul and Silas were released, and the jailer and his entire household were converted to Christianity.

On several other occasions, Paul was persecuted. Because he saw the big picture of God's purpose and so understood that God can turn bad into good, he never whined. Instead, he repeatedly turned his persecutions into opportunities to share the gospel. While he was in shackles, Paul told the truth to a lynch mob, the leading Jewish religious body in Jerusalem, two Roman governors, and a king. None of these good opportunities would have happened without the bad event of his imprisonment. Also, as a prisoner Paul had the time to write several epistles he might not have written otherwise (Philippians, Ephesians, Colossians, Philemon, 2 Timothy, and Titus). On top of that, he led many of his guards to Christ.

Because the unique position of imprisonment enabled him to share the gospel, Paul actually rejoiced that good had come out of bad. From prison, he wrote to the Philippians the following:

> *Now I want you to know, brothers, that what has happened to me has really served to advance the gospel.*
>
> PHILIPPIANS 1:12

Paul understood that imprisonment is bad. But God used it for great good not only for him or the first-century believers, but also for the whole world. No wonder he recorded Romans 8:28, a great promise of God's ability to turn bad into good.

Bad to Good in the Twenty-First Century

It was early in the morning when Pastor Jamal's phone began to ring. Everyone had the same questions and the same bad news. Had he seen the sidewalks? Did he know what had happened? Did he have any idea who did it?

His young church was only a little over a year and a half old and was still working hard to be a positive voice for Christ on campus. Now this happened: Someone had taken chalk and written all over the sidewalks of the campus of Ohio State University the condemning words, "New Life Church Hates Gays!"

What do you do when falsely accused and helpless to do anything about it? You pray. So Jamal and others turned their problems into prayers, and God quickly turned evil into good. Whoever wrote the lying words must have been infuriated when they learned what soon happened.

First, in a feature article in the weekly student newspaper, the church was given the opportunity to set the record straight. No, they had not written that message on the sidewalk. The truth was they loved all people. They did not condone homosexuality, but they did not hate gays. They existed to help students find deeper meaning in life through a personal relationship with God.

Second, because their church name was smeared on the sidewalks, the church was featured in the school newspaper. This created a buzz in the student body and afforded New Life Church a presence on campus that would have taken them years to attain otherwise. Now everyone knew there was a new church on campus.

Third, the publicity drew a reporter with a camera to the church's service the following Sunday. There the pastor addressed the issue in a gracious and loving way, and guests witnessed vibrant Christianity in action.

Fourth, it rained the next day, washing the sidewalks clean. But this did not happen before God had turned evil into great good. Yay, God![1]

A *Final Encouragement*

If God could turn Joseph's big mess into greater good, He can do it for you. If He could turn Paul's imprisonment to something positive, He will do it for you. You don't have to be perfect or one of the spiritual superelite. You just need to love God. That's the promise.

Note

1. Story used by permission of Jamal Jivanjee. Jamal is the lead pastor of Newlife–OSU, an exciting young church on the campus of the Ohio State University.

6

God's Promise of Providential Provision

PHILIPPIANS 4:19

We all have material needs. Food, shelter, and clothing are right there at the top of the list. Following close behind are things like furniture, drapes, sheets, blankets, and towels. It's great to have a job and a means of transportation to get there. Gas money and car insurance are important. Money for books, an occasional meal out, and a few toys for the kids is very nice. Health insurance is a big one. So is money for retirement. On and on the list goes.

I don't know what you really need or what you can live without, but God does, and He promises to provide all of your needs.

> *And my God will meet all your needs according to his glorious riches in Christ Jesus.*
>
> PHILIPPIANS 4:19

God promises to provide us with the necessities of life. This is a reassuring promise, because God is a reliable source. We need not worry if He can come through. He promises to provide for our needs according to His riches in glory.

Now, if I promised to meet all your needs according to my glorious riches, it would not be such a great promise. This is because I have limited riches, and the ones I have are not all that glorious. If your need exceeded the amount of money in my checking account, my promise would mean little and you'd be in trouble.

But God's promise to meet your needs is an awesome encouragement. God can meet your needs and everyone else's, because He has infinite riches in Christ Jesus. Money is no obstacle to God. If He wanted, He could snap his fingers and bury you in hundred-dollar bills (which sounds like a lot of fun)! He could blink His eyes and surround you with gold, silver, and diamonds (also fun). Believe me, God is able to supply all of your needs.

The Condition for God's Provision

Paul promised the Philippians that God would meet their needs because of their previous generosity to those in God's service. The promise of Philippians 4:19 follows on the heels of his thanking them in verses 14–18 for giving to his needs. They had sent a care package to him when he was in a prison in Rome.

They were not wealthy people giving out of their abundance. They were persecuted Christians, living in a town in the midst of an economic depression. Yet when the opportunity was presented to give to Paul, they did it.

God wants to pull our eyes off ourselves and focus them on others. We must not forget that others need us. When we meet the needs of others, God assumes the obligation to meet our needs. The point is this: The key to receiving is giving.

The Key to Receiving Is Giving

Philippians 4 is not the only place God promises to provide the needs of those who give to others. A few of my favorite promises include these:

"Give, and it will be given to you. A good measure, pressed down, shaken together and running over, will be poured into your lap. For with the measure you use, it will be measured to you."

Luke 6:38

He who is kind to the poor lends to the Lord, and he will reward him for what he has done.

Proverbs 19:17

He who gives to the poor will lack nothing.

Proverbs 28:27

Seventeenth-Century Generosity

In the latter part of the seventeenth century, August H. Francke founded an orphanage to care for homeless children. One day, when Francke desperately needed funds to carry on his work, a destitute Christian widow came to his door begging for a gold coin. Because of his financial situation, he politely but regretfully told her he couldn't help her.

Disheartened, the woman began to weep. Moved by her tears, Francke asked her to wait while he went to his room to pray. After seeking God's guidance, he felt that the Holy Spirit wanted him to change his mind. Trusting the Lord to meet his own needs, he gave her the money.

Two mornings later, he received a letter of thanks from the widow. She explained that because of his generosity she had asked the Lord to shower the orphanage with gifts.

That same day Francke received twelve gold coins from

a wealthy lady and two more from a friend in Sweden. He thought he had been amply rewarded for helping the widow, but he was soon informed that the orphanage was to receive five hundred gold pieces from the estate of Prince Lodewyk Van Wurtenburg! Francke found that God meets the needs of those who meet the needs of others.

A Twenty-First-Century Provision

I love stories about God providing for His believers; I could tell dozens of them. However, as I was writing this chapter, I was convicted that I had recently been lax in living by faith. Apart from tithing, I had not given much away lately and very little to the poor. As I was thinking about my lack of extra-generous giving, my phone rang. On the other end was a young man who had come to America from Africa for an education and a job. Yet things had not worked out for him. He had no work visa and was in desperate straits. His only income came from singing in churches. He told me the next day he was hoping to meet with a lawyer who, for a small fee, would help him get his visa.

Without thinking, I said, "I can't talk now; I'm late for an appointment. But I'll drop by and see you tonight. I have some money for you." Excitedly, he gave me his address and said he'd be waiting. When I hung up the phone, a wave of regret swept over me.

"Uh-oh," I thought. "What money will I give him?" I had just left a meeting where I took a 50 percent pay cut because I believed God wanted me to follow a new direction in my ministry. I have three teenage boys. They are expensive just to feed, let alone provide everything else they require. I would need all the money I could get. Besides, I had been on the go nonstop for two weeks, and that night was to be my first night home in a long time. Then I remembered that the week before I had earned a couple of hundred dollars by selling my books at a pastor's conference. I thought, "I'll give him that money."

As the time approached to visit him, I felt more and more exhausted. I thought of several good excuses for not going, but no legitimate reasons. So I dragged myself out the door and drove across town toward the apartment complex where the young man was staying with friends.

I got lost several times trying to find the right apartment building in the dark. Eventually I found the building but did not have a key to get through the secured door. I did not know the name of the person he was staying with, and I had forgotten his phone number.

I went back to my car and prayed. "Lord if you want me to see this man and give him the money, I need to get into the building. If you don't provide me a way within the next five minutes, I am going home and going to bed."

After a few minutes, a beat-up car pulled up near the door of the building. A scraggly young man carrying a case of beer got out. I jumped out of my car and walked to the entrance. I hoped to nonchalantly walk to the door and get inside before it could swing closed in my face.

I missed it by a tenth of a second.

"Lord, help me," I whispered as I banged on the door.

The young man turned and saw me. He shook his head no.

"Wait," I said, "I need your help."

He just smirked.

"I am a pastor, and I need to visit a man on the third floor. He is from Africa, and I don't think he understands how these security systems work."

He glared into my eyes. Then he opened the door for me

and walked off, shaking his head.

I bolted up the stairs and banged on the door. My friend met me and let me in. He began to tell me how glad he was to see me and again recounted all he had gone through. After a while, I couldn't keep my eyes open. So I stood up and handed him the two hundred dollars. He hugged me, danced around, and walked me to my car. I went home and went to bed. I was glad I had been able to give the money to someone who needed it more than I did.

The next morning my phone rang. A pastor who had been at the conference the week before was on the line. He had bought my book and had read it. Now he wanted to order a copy for each of his church leaders. He said that above my costs, he'd send me two hundred dollars.

$943.00!

As a pastor, I am obligated to teach the Word of God, even the parts I do not necessarily like. A few years ago when my children were small and money was quite tight, I was struggling to write a Sunday morning teaching on the subject of giving to God.

Later that week I received a letter in the mail from a Virginia bank in a town where my wife and I had lived when we first got married. It stated that they were closing my old account and sending me the money. Enclosed with the letter was a check. I was certain I had closed all my accounts with that bank when we had moved to Ohio. So I called the bank, and they said that the money was definitely mine.

I jumped up, ran into my study, and yanked down our home budget book. My heart pounded. I was eager to see exactly how much we had given above our tithe that year. We had given $943.00.

Slowly I turned the check over to read the amount. It was $943.00!

A Final Encouragement

The key to receiving is giving. God can and will meet your needs. He has promised to do this, and many believers have found it to be true. You can, too.

7

God's Promise of Eternal Life

John 3:16

If you died today, are you sure you would go to heaven? What would you say if God were to ask you, "Why should I allow you into heaven?" You would want to be confident you had the right answers to those two questions.

Wrestling with Doubt

If you had asked Thomas those questions, he probably would have been stumped. With the high-powered mind of an engineer, Thomas wrestled with doubt. He would never think of committing to something lightly. He needed evidence. He needed to be sure.

This man enjoyed the rare privilege of being one of Jesus Christ's twelve closest traveling companions. With his own eyes, Thomas had seen Jesus do what no other man had ever done. He witnessed Jesus miraculously healing the sick, feeding the hungry, freeing the demonized, calming the storm, and even raising the dead. Such displays of deity kept Thomas's doubts at bay. He was starting to truly believe that Jesus was Messiah. However, his confidence was violently crushed one dark afternoon.

Jesus, the man who claimed to be the Messiah, had been arrested, beaten, and tried. Beyond that, Jesus had appeared to helplessly allow evil men to drive spikes through his hands and feet into a cross.

Thomas's mind could not accept the data. It did not make sense.

"If Jesus really was God, why was he powerless to stop this brutal injustice? No God would allow mere men to take his life. So maybe Jesus really wasn't Messiah. Maybe it was some sort of magic."

Thomas's old friend Doubt dogged his thoughts and flooded his heart. He began to wonder why he had wasted those three years following a fake. Then some of Thomas's friends claimed to have seen Jesus resurrected from the dead.

"Right," Thomas thought. "I'll believe that when I see it for myself and not a second before. Actually, seeing it is not enough. I'll believe it when I literally stick my fingers in those nail marks in his hands. I will not be fooled."

Thomas Accepts Reality

One week later, Thomas was eating with some of his friends. They had kept the door locked because they were afraid that the same people who had arrested and killed Jesus might do the same to them. Suddenly the bizarre occurred. Jesus walked right into the room through the closed, locked door as though it was nothing out of the ordinary. He even smiled and greeted them. Then Jesus went to Thomas and said:

> *"Put your finger here; see my hands. Reach out your hand and put it into my side. Stop doubting and believe."*
>
> John 20:27

That was more than enough for Thomas. All his doubt was gone when he touched those nail-pierced hands of Jesus. He looked at Jesus and said, "My Lord and my God!"

Then Jesus told him:

"Because you have seen me, you have believed; blessed are those who have not seen and yet have believed."

JOHN 20:29

Your Greatest Need

Your greatest need is for eternal life. It is not just your greatest spiritual need; it is your greatest need, period. Whether one thousand years from now or this very second, the most significant issue in your life is whether you have eternal life.

"For God so loved the world that He gave His only begotten Son, that whoever believes in Him should not perish but have everlasting life."

JOHN 3:16 NKJV

God really loves you. You are more than a random gathering of highly evolved atoms. You are a person God loves and for whom Jesus died. You are someone God wants to spend eternity with. You are a candidate for the gift of eternal life.

The Bad News about the Good News

The good news is that God wants to give you eternal life. The bad news is that without it you are in big trouble. The Bible is very clear about our condition without God.

Fact: We have all committed sins and fallen short of God's glory.

For all have sinned and fall short of the glory of God.

ROMANS 3:23

The word used for "sinned" in Romans 6:23 means to miss the mark. It was a first-century archery term that described failing to hit the bull's-eye. The moral, spiritual bull's-eye is God's glory. It is perfect holiness. Unfortunately, none of us are perfect, none holy. Somewhere along the way we have lied, or stolen, or cheated, or sworn, or failed to treat someone with love, or lost our temper, or gossiped, or slandered. We have been greedy, or jealous, or envious, or lustful, or lazy. Even when we try hard to be good, we just can't consistently pull it off.

Let's say that getting into heaven requires that we hit the bull's-eye of righteousness. Now, maybe you have lived a better life than I have and the arrow of your morality hits closer to the bull's-eye than mine. But the bottom line is this: Unless you are perfect, you have sinned; you have missed the bull's-eye.

Fact: Sin has a steep price tag.

For the wages of sin is death.

Romans 6:23

The price tag of sin is death. When the Bible uses the term "death" here, the concept is separation. Physical death is the separation of one's soul from the body. Spiritual death is the separation of the soul from God. Eternal death is separation of a soul from God forever.

If we don't have eternal life, we look forward to eternal death. We face an eternity of separation from God. God is perfectly holy. We are not. Our sin creates a great chasm separating us from God. On our own, we have no hope of bridging the chasm to get to God and eternal life.

But Jesus did it for us.

The Good News about the Bad News

Fact: Jesus never sinned.

This fact makes Jesus unique in all of history and in the entire universe. As the Son of God, He is sinless. Only Jesus lived a perfectly moral, righteous, holy life. Only Jesus hit the bull's-eye of righteousness. Only Jesus fulfilled the glory of God. Only Jesus never sinned. Only Jesus did not deserve to die.

Fact: Jesus died to pay for our sins.

I am a Christian and would never consider being a Muslim, a Buddhist, or anything else because Jesus provides the only way to get to God. When Jesus died for my sins, He bridged the gap between God and me, thereby making it possible for me to receive eternal life.

I deserve to experience death. He did not deserve to experience death. Yet because God loves me, Jesus died for me. Now I have eternal life—a new spiritual relationship in God's family that begins at the moment of salvation. Here are the facts about eternal life:

- *It's new.* Jesus also called it being "born again" or "born anew."
- *It's spiritual.* It is not a physical birth, but a birth of the spirit.
- *It's a relationship.* Prior to salvation, our relationship with God is distant because of sin. He is under no obligation to bless us or hear our prayers. We are called enemies of God. Our sin is viewed as a barrier

between God and us. Yet after we are saved, the barrier is torn down. We are born anew into God's family. He is no longer our judge declaring us guilty but our Father declaring us loved.

- *It begins at the moment of saving faith.* The clock of eternity does not begin the moment we die; it begins the moment we believe. The clock of eternal life begins the moment we are saved, born again, not the moment we die physically.

"You Gotta Believe"

The condition for receiving eternal life is belief in Christ. We believe *in* Him, not facts *about* Him. It is not enough to believe there was a man named Jesus who once lived in Israel, or that Jesus was a good man, or that Jesus was the Son of God, or even that Jesus was the Son of God who died on the cross to pay for sins. We must believe *in* Him. Many people believe things *about* Jesus but do not have eternal life. James 2:19 states that even demons believe and tremble, but they certainly do not have eternal life. In order to have eternal life, you must believe *in* Christ. What does this mean? The following story will help make it clear.

You Must Get in the Wheelbarrow

One summer vacation, our family visited Niagara Falls. The falls span 1,060 feet and stand at a height of 176 feet. 150,000 gallons of water pour over the falls every second. They are so large you can hear the water pounding over them several miles away.

Across one of the main streets of Niagara is a statue of a man on a tightrope. His name was Jean Francois Gravelet, the great Blondin. He was a professional artist and showman trained in the great tradition of the European circus. At age thirty-one, he came to America and announced that he would cross the gorge of the Niagara River on a tightrope.

On June 30, 1859, Blondin became the first man to walk across Niagara Falls on a tightrope. But he did more than that. He eventually crossed the falls several times in a variety of ways: blindfolded, on a bicycle, with his hands and feet manacled, and even with his manager on his back.

Yet none of these stunts compares with Blondin's greatest feat. One day Blondin put a wheelbarrow on his tightrope and asked the crowd if they believed he could wheel it across. They yelled, "We believe!"

He wheeled it across and back. Then he called out, "Who believes I can put a man in my wheelbarrow and wheel him across?"

The excited crowd yelled, "We believe."

So he looked into the faces of that crowd and said, "Who will be first?"[1]

Blondin was not asking the crowd what they believed *about* him and his wheelbarrow. He was asking if they believed *in* him. Eternal life is not a matter of standing on the sidelines with nice beliefs *about* Jesus. It is a matter of believing *in* Him. You will never cross over into eternal life until you get in the wheelbarrow.

If you were in the crowd that day, you could cross the Niagara by having the faith to get in the wheelbarrow. In the same way, you receive eternal life by having the faith to get in Jesus' wheelbarrow. That is, you must have faith in Him as the complete payment for your sins.

I wonder, have you ever really believed *in* Jesus? God loves you so much that He sent His Son to bridge the gorge to provide the only way for you to experience eternal life.

A Final Encouragement

If you died today, are you sure you would experience eternal life in heaven? If not, you can be. Do you need to get into Jesus' wheelbarrow? If so, it is a matter of faith. Would you express your faith right now by calling upon Jesus to be your Savior? You can do it by honestly praying this simple prayer:

> *Dear Jesus,*
>
> *I admit that I am not perfect. I have sinned. Forgive me. I do not deserve eternal life. I have fallen short of Your standard of righteousness. I admit I need a Savior. I believe that You took my place and died for my sin. Now, I personally commit myself to You. I'm getting in the wheelbarrow. I trust You and You alone as my Savior.*

Note

1. "The First Tightrope Walker, Jean Francois Blondin" by the Niagara Parks Commission in Niagara, http://www.niagara-info.com/historic.htm#Section1c (August 25, 2005).

8

God's Promise of Sufficient Grace

2 CORINTHIANS 12:9

On August 18, 1991, I woke up with a horrible case of the flu, and it never completely went away. I lost eighteen pounds in three weeks. I felt continual pain in my joints and muscles. Any inkling of cold air made it all the worse.

Then there was the giant headache that refused to go away. Also, I found that I was suddenly allergic to all sorts of new things. Catching a whiff of perfume was like getting hit in the head by a two-by-four. The smell of freshly cut grass made me feel awful all over.

Frustratingly, my cognitive capacities would randomly short-circuit. I could form words in my mind but had great difficulty getting them to come out of my mouth. This is not a good thing for a pastor who speaks in four services every weekend.

Strangely, about five o'clock every evening, I would get a sore throat and begin to feel waves of despair crashing on the beach of my soul. Because I ached so much, it was difficult to sleep for more than a few hours at a time.

Yet I gladly would have kept all of those maladies to be rid of the constant, devastating fatigue. Formerly a morning person, I woke up exhausted every day, and this only got worse as the day wore on. There were times when the highlight of my day was to crawl down the hall to the bathroom. Many nights I'd lay in bed concentrating all my strength just to turn over.

At that same time, my three boys were all under the age

of five. They could not understand why Dad would not play with them like he used to, why he could not go out and make a snowman.

Meanwhile, my church needed my leadership. Yet I barely had the energy to get to the office, let alone provide significant leadership.

Worst of all was the guilt. My wife needed me to help around the house and with the children. Yet it was all I could do to take care of myself and try to keep working. I hated to see my exhaustion wearing her out.

I suffered like this for ten months before I sought help. I kept thinking that I'd wake up the next day feeling better, but I never did. I went through a wearisome battery of tests, doctors, and diagnoses.

Eventually I was diagnosed with chronic fatigue immuno deficiency syndrome—CFIDS—an illness few people understood and no one was sure how to treat.

I was frustrated at being the slave of my pain and fatigue. I was a goal-oriented person not able to pursue any goal beyond survival. I was perturbed and sad because I did not have the strength to get off the couch to play with my boys. I was so disappointed to see how my fatigue was exhausting my wife.

I hate to admit that my frustration was focused on the Lord. Day after day, I asked for deliverance, for an explanation, for a time frame for my agony. Yet day after day, week after week, month after month, the only response I received from God was silence—deafening silence.

I am glad that I did not quit reading my Bible or praying. Several encouraging Bible promises and personalities kept me going. I wore out the book of Job, finding some comfort that his adversity was greater than mine and that his story had a happy ending. I practically memorized the story of Joseph's shocking kidnapping, enslavement, and false imprisonment. I found strength reading of innocent David, running for his life from Saul and eventually becoming king. I read his journal, the book of Psalms, over and over again.

However, I was especially encouraged by the words of the apostle Paul. Even though he experienced extreme sufferings, he only benefited from them. He never let his pain distort his perspective or steal his joy. He obviously had discovered a secret I needed to learn, a promise I needed to apply.

Paul's Battle with a Thorn

Near the end of his second letter to the church at Corinth, Paul pulls back the veil and gives us a wonderful glimpse into his interior life. In doing so, he reveals his battle with what he refers to as a thorn in the flesh.

> *To keep me from becoming conceited because of these surpassingly great revelations, there was given me a thorn in my flesh, a messenger of Satan, to torment me. Three times I pleaded with the Lord to take it away from me. But he said to me, "My grace is sufficient for you, for my power is made perfect in weakness." Therefore I will boast all the more gladly about my weaknesses, so that Christ's power may rest on me. That is why, for Christ's sake, I delight in weaknesses, in insults, in hardships, in persecutions, in difficulties. For when I am weak, then I am strong.*
>
> 2 Corinthians 12:7–10

There is much for the soul in these four verses of Scripture. I was encouraged by several discoveries.

Even Paul experienced "a thorn in [his] flesh, a messenger of Satan" (12:7). No one is exempt from suffering. It is an unavoidable aspect of the human condition.

God can use such thorns to restrain us from pride (12:7). Since pride blocks our relationship with God (James 4:6), anything that blunts the edge of pride is beneficial.

Even a spiritual giant like Paul received unanswered prayers. (12:8). You and I may have thorns, but this does not necessarily mean we are not spiritual.

Such thorns remind us that life ultimately is not about us (12:9). Life is about the Lord, His grace, and His power.

Thorns help us boast in and depend upon God (12:10). They also help us find our strength in the Lord (2 Corinthians 12:9).

The fact that the nature of Paul's thorn is unspecified makes his experience applicable to each of us at our point of pain. Scholars love to debate what Paul was talking about when he spoke of his thorn in the flesh. Was it a physical problem with his eyes? Was it a demon? Was it a divorce by an unbelieving wife?

We don't know the answer to this, because the Bible does not say. We are not supposed to know. Whether our battle is physical, spiritual, or relational in nature is not the issue. The issue is that God's grace is sufficient. His grace is sufficient for any and every thorn in anyone's flesh.

Grace Is Found in Weakness

> *"My grace is sufficient for you, for my power is made perfect in weakness."*
>
> 2 Corinthians 12:9

Paul asked God to remove the thorn. God said, "No." Paul asked again. God said, "No." The third time Paul received the same answer, "No." Why is this?

God said, "No," because God wanted Paul to learn that His grace was sufficient *even when* Paul suffered with a thorn in the flesh. God's grace is not just available on the easy days. It is especially real when it is needed the most. God wanted Paul and countless others through Paul's words to realize the reality of God's grace. It runs deeper, reaches higher, stretches broader, and lasts longer than any thorn Satan can ever send our way.

Our defining moment as unbelievers occurred when we understood that God's grace is greater than any sin. Our joyous breakthrough as Christians occurs when we understand that God's grace is greater than any thorn.

I have served as a pastor of God's flock for many years and have had the privilege of ministering to people when they had great need, severe pain, and deep sorrow. Many times I have walked out of a hospital room, a funeral home, a cemetery, or even a police station and thought, "Wow. A normal person would be knocked out cold by this agony. I have just left the presence of a saint who has discovered God's secret of sufficient grace."

A Final Encouragement

I don't know specifically why God is allowing that unremoved thorn in your life. However, I do know that His grace is sufficient to see you through. I also know that His grace is able to use the pain and suffering caused by your thorn to wonderfully bless your life. Trust Him.

9

God's Promise of Supernatural Support

2 Chronicles 16:9

There are times when waves of problems threaten to capsize our small boat. Or, to use another image, there are times when troubles hound us like a pack of angry dogs. These are times when we face an impossible set of circumstances and need supreme strength; otherwise, we are not going to make it.

I have three quick questions for you to consider at such times:

1. How big is God? The answer: Big enough!
2. How strong is God? The answer: Strong enough!
3. How do you get God to show His might on your behalf? The answer: It is a matter of the heart.

Just ask Asa.

Holding Back on God

Asa was a prince, the son of Abijah, king of Judah. In his father, Asa saw a man who struggled to give the Lord all of his heart. At times Abijah did well. He rebuked those in idolatry and refused to turn his back on God. When he faced a battle, he completely depended on the Lord, and God blessed him for it (2 Chronicles 13:6–18). Yet on other occasions he was a disloyal, halfhearted follower of the Lord who kept idols in the land and held back on God. Eventually God withheld His support, and Abijah's reign was filled with war (1 Kings 15:3). In a sense, he was one man with two hearts. Most of us can identify with him.

All Out for God

After observing his father's struggles, Asa launched his reign as king with a wholehearted commitment to the Lord. Beyond merely rebuking those with idols, he tore down altars to foreign gods and cut down their images. He commanded his people to worship and obey the Lord. When the Ethiopian army came to invade his land, Asa turned his problem into prayer. God liked what He saw in Asa's heart and supported him with a glorious, miraculous triumph (2 Chronicles 14:11–13).

The Lord promised to continue His supernatural support of Asa as long as Asa maintained his wholehearted devotion to the Lord (2 Chronicles 15:2, 7). And Asa did this. He destroyed idols, rebuilt altars, gave gifts, and made sacrifices. He also led his people to pledge their wholehearted allegiance to the Lord. So the Lord protected them.

> *They entered into a covenant to seek the* Lord, *the God of their fathers, with all their heart and soul. . . . They took an oath to the* Lord *with loud acclamation, with shouting and with trumpets and horns. All Judah rejoiced about the oath because they had sworn it wholeheartedly. They sought God eagerly, and he was found by them. So the* Lord *gave them rest on every side. . . . Asa's heart was fully committed to the* Lord *all his life.*
>
> 2 Chronicles 15:12–17

Asa gave God his whole heart, and God gave Asa His full support. It was a sweet arrangement as long as it lasted.

Wholehearted No More

It was simple, really. As long as Asa was totally committed, the Lord blessed him with supernatural support and he experienced victory, peace, and prosperity. But as time went by, Asa let his defenses down and allowed outside pressure to push him to drop his all-out commitment to God.

This is how it happened. Judah, Asa's kingdom, lived in constant military threat by Israel—a part of the Jewish nation that had turned from God years earlier. Instead of living in wholehearted dependence on the Lord, Asa came up with a scheme. He would persuade the nation to the north of Israel, Aram, to attack Israel for him, thereby drawing their attention from Judah. So he sent the king of Aram money to attack Israel. Initially, Asa's plot worked. But God was not pleased. He sent a sobering message to Asa:

> *"Because you relied on the king of Aram and not on the* LORD *your God, the army of the king of Aram has escaped from your hand. . . . When you relied on the* LORD*, he delivered them into your hand."*
>
> 2 CHRONICLES 16:7–8

God told him that the small success of his scheme had cost him the opportunity to do away with his enemies once and for all. God also reminded him that when he previously relied on the Lord, he won great victories. Now the hand of the Lord's protection and peace would be removed, and Judah would have to contend with both Israel and Aram.

Then God made a piercing observation and a stunning promise. Read this carefully in the translations given:

> *"For the eyes of the LORD range throughout the earth to strengthen those whose hearts are fully committed to him. You have done a foolish thing, and from now on you will be at war."*
>
> 2 CHRONICLES 16:9

> *"For the eyes of the LORD move to and fro throughout the earth that He may strongly support those whose heart is completely His."*
>
> 2 CHRONICLES 16:9 NASB

> *"For the eyes of the LORD run to and fro throughout the whole earth, to show Himself strong on behalf of those whose heart is loyal to Him. In this you have done foolishly; therefore from now on you shall have wars."*
>
> 2 CHRONICLES 16:9 NKJV

Good News: Strength on Our Behalf

The promise is this: God will strongly support, strengthen, and show Himself strong for those whose hearts are wholly committed to Him. Wow! That is good news. Simply put, God's promise to us is that His supernatural strength will work on our behalf.

Since nothing is too big for God, and nothing is too complicated for Him to understand, then no problem is outside His capabilities to resolve. Think of it. The almighty, all-knowing, awesome God is on our side. He will help us. He will hold us up. He will roll up His sleeves and flex His muscles on our behalf. It does not get any better than that!

No problem you are facing is too big for Him. No situation you are in is too complex. He is big enough. He can handle it. He is God. He will give you His full support.

What a relief! This promise is such an encouragement. It lifts our burdens.

There have been times in my life when the Lord was obviously supporting me. Knotted issues, massive problems, and impossible situations were resolved because God was clearing the way. I also have experienced times when I was trying to handle it all in my strength and wisdom. There was no powerful hand pushing the obstacles aside. There was no all-knowing mind solving the problem. The results were not pretty.

Anytime He chooses, God can accomplish everything and anything better, bigger, and faster than we can. He is God. We are not. We need Him. The extent to which we trust in, depend on, and commit to Him is the extent to which we see His strength working on our behalf.

There's a Catch

Look again at the promise: "The eyes of the Lord range throughout the earth to strengthen those whose hearts are fully committed to him."

Such a sensational promise has a stringent requirement. God's full support of us is dependent on our full commitment to Him. The promise is that the Lord God is looking to strongly support those whose hearts are fully committed, completely devoted, and absolutely loyal to Him. He will do His part *if* we do our part. This means we must have no other gods crowding our hearts. We cannot put our ultimate reliance on persons or things other than God. And we cannot hold back any portion of our hearts from Him.

Yet sometimes our commitment to Him wavers. As a result, His strong support on our behalf disappears. Then trouble comes. Just ask Asa.

God's Support Will Abandon the Heart That Abandons Him

> *For the eyes of the* LORD *range throughout the earth to strengthen those whose hearts are fully committed to him. You have done a foolish thing, and from now on you will be at war."*
>
> 2 CHRONICLES 16:9

Instead of seeking the Lord's aid, Asa had given his trust to the king of Aram. This was foolish. No king, especially the king of Aram, could possibly surpass, let alone compare to, God. Foolishly, Asa acted as though he did not need God, so God left him alone. Without the protecting hand of God, peace was forfeited and problems set in. Unlike the early days of Asa's reign, the last years of his reign were marked with war (16:9). He was full of anger (16:10). And his feet were afflicted with disease (16:11). But it need not be that way for us.

Supernatural Support Today

The other day my good friend Pastor Chris Brown told me how God proved Himself strong on his behalf as he launched a brand-new church. This is his story:

On the first day of July of 1999, two committed staff members, a core group of twenty-five adults, and myself were planning to plant New Life Community Church. Our plan was to meet in a local elementary school, and we were discussing an interesting dilemma. How do we transport all the equipment and materials for a church worship gathering each week, fifty-two weeks a year?

The answer was found in an ingenious system that included a twenty-four-foot trailer, fifteen cases, and a Suburban truck. Wonderful! Not quite. We needed forty-five thousand dollars for the system, of which twelve thousand dollars was due as a deposit by the first week of July. Great. . .we only had two thousand dollars in the bank.

After some discussion, our entire group agreed: this wasn't a want, it was a need, and we needed to order the system. So we did the only logical thing—we dropped to our knees and prayed, asking God for ten thousand dollars by the end of the week.

We ended the gathering and I started the drive home, trying to figure out a way to ask my wealthiest friends for money. But God had His own plans.

The first clue came when I stopped by the post office box and discovered a check for one thousand dollars. "Okay," I thought, "we're on the way, but what about the rest? We still need nine thousand dollars." Sunday night I returned home to find an envelope with my name on it. As I opened the envelope, it contained nothing but a single check. No note, no explanation, just a check. . .for nine thousand dollars!

I gave thanks to God. I knew New Life was God's church from that day forward, and that the Lord was with us and would strongly support us. We simply needed to remain committed to and dependent upon Him.[1]

A Final Encouragement

When we commit everything of ourselves to God, He commits all of Himself to us. This is a great deal! He will strongly support those who are dedicated to Him. He did it for Asa, Chris Brown, New Life Community Church, and countless others. He will do it for you.

Note

1. Used by permission of Chris Brown. Chris is the lead pastor of New Life Community Church, an outstanding young church in Canal Winchester, Ohio.

10

God's Promise of Full Forgiveness

1 JOHN 1:9

It's an all-too-familiar story. Israel's King David was in his midlife crisis. After years of working hard to follow God and to establish the kingdom of Israel, David let down his defenses. Like too many leaders, he began to believe his press clippings. He did not think he needed to be accountable to anyone or obey the same rules as everyone else. Predictably, such arrogance set him up for a downfall.

David, as king, should have been out leading his nation. Instead, he stayed home. Bored and restless, he wandered on the terrace of the roof of his palace one night. There temptation awaited him in the shapely form of another man's wife. Arrogance and desire welled up within him. Lust overpowered his heart, and he took steps to commit adultery with Bathsheba.

But it did not stop there. Pride took the upper hand, and David attempted to cover his sin by having Bathsheba's husband killed. After that, he denied his sin by going on as though nothing had happened.

But something had happened—something big, bad, and significant.

David had sinned.

Guilt and shame don't just go away on their own. For David, they grew stronger day by day. His inner anger and disappointment with himself bred deep depression. Unresolved guilt hung over him like a black cloud. His once-passionate relationship with God was only a shell. Silently, David was drowning in a dark sea of guilt and shame. Later he recalled that draining, dreadful, painful period with these words:

> *When I kept silent, my bones wasted away through my groaning all day long. For day and night your hand was heavy upon me; my strength was sapped as in the heat of summer.*
>
> Psalm 32:3–4

You Are the Man

Finally, God stopped waiting for David to act and took things into His own hands. In His great mercy and grace, the Lord sent Nathan, a prophet, to confront David about his sins. I imagine that Nathan fully expected to be killed for his obedience. After all, if David had Bathsheba's husband killed, what would he do to a man who confronted him with his sin?

Nathan was very wise in his approach. Rather than sticking his bony prophet's finger in David's face, he told David a story of a poor man who owned just one beloved lamb and of a rich man who had many sheep. When a guest dropped in to visit, the rich man wanted to feed him well. But rather than use one of his lambs to feed the man, he took the poor man's lamb.

Fortunately, the story struck a cord deep in David's heart. Filled with righteous indignation, David immediately condemned the rich man to death.

Now Nathan had David where he wanted him. Turning to face David, Nathan confronted him with his sin.

> *"You are the man! This is what the LORD, the God of Israel, says: 'I anointed you king over Israel, and I delivered you from the hand of Saul. I gave your master's house to you, and your master's wives into your arms. I gave you the house of Israel and Judah. And if all this had been too little, I would have given you even more. Why did you despise the word of the LORD by doing what is evil in his eyes? You struck down Uriah the Hittite with the sword and took his wife to be your own. You killed him with the sword of the Ammonites.'"*
>
> 2 SAMUEL 12:7–9

At that moment, David had three options. He could blow up in anger at Nathan, and at God, for declaring him guilty and pestering him about his sin. He could give up and melt away in depression and defeat. Or he could own up to his sin and seek to make things right with God.

Fortunately, for himself and for us, David did the latter. He admitted his sin and found forgiveness.

Lord, Have Mercy

Later David reviewed that defining moment. His thoughts and prayer are found in Psalm 51. Read slowly through the beginning of this psalm, and note carefully the caption.

> *A psalm of David. When the prophet Nathan came to him after David had committed adultery with Bathsheba.*
>
> *Have mercy on me, O God, according to your unfailing love; according to your great compassion blot out my transgressions. Wash away all my iniquity and cleanse me from*

> *my sin. For I know my transgressions, and my sin is always before me. Against you, you only, have I sinned and done what is evil in your sight, so that you are proved right when you speak and justified when you judge. . . . Cleanse me with hyssop, and I will be clean; wash me, and I will be whiter than snow. Let me hear joy and gladness; let the bones you have crushed rejoice. Hide your face from my sins and blot out all my iniquity. Create in me a pure heart, O God, and renew a steadfast spirit within me.*
>
> PSALM 51:1–10

The bad news is that David and his family would deal with the deep scars of that great sin for the rest of their lives (see 2 Samuel 12:10–19). The good news is that God heard him, forgave him, and restored him. Later David recorded the tremendous happiness that was unleashed in his heart when his sin was forgiven. His resulting song of experienced joy is Psalm 32. Eugene Petersen in *The Message* renders this psalm with these words:

> *Count yourself lucky, how happy you must be—you get a fresh start, your slate's wiped clean. Count yourself lucky—GOD holds nothing against you and you're holding nothing back from him. When I kept it all inside, my bones turned to powder, my words became daylong groans. The pressure never let up; all the juices of my life dried up. Then I let it all out; I said, "I'll make a clean breast of my failures to GOD." Suddenly the pressure was gone—my guilt dissolved, my sin disappeared.*
>
> PSALM 32:1–5 THE MESSAGE

David's story and the corresponding psalms are a great example of God's encouraging promise of forgiveness. The apostle John recorded it succinctly with these words:

> *If we confess our sins, he is faithful and just and will forgive us our sins and purify us from all unrighteousness.*
>
> 1 John 1:9

If We Confess Our Sins

The word *confess* means "to say the same thing," which means that we say the same thing about our sin that God says. When we confess our sin, we don't call it a mistake, a mess-up, an error, or misbehavior. We call it what it is, sin. We agree that it is wrong. We concur with the fact that it must be forgiven, it needs to be washed off our record, and it has to be purified from our hearts.

David was forgiven because he was truly sorry for his sin and meant business with God about being cleansed of it. He was not merely sorry that he had been caught or that he would be punished. He was sorry that he had disobeyed and hurt God.

All sin hurts God, not merely adultery and murder. Worry, doubt, laziness, lust, greed, jealousy, envy, bitterness, resentment, lying, cheating, deceit, gossip, slander, hatred, harshness, arrogance, and pride all break the heart of God.

Look back at Psalm 51. Notice the way David heaped up his brokenhearted requests as he confessed his sin. Hear the sorrow in his voice as he cried, "Have mercy on me. . . ; blot out my transgressions. Wash away all my iniquity and cleanse me from my sin. . . . ; Cleanse me with hyssop. . . . ; wash me. . . . ; Hide your face from my sins and blot out all my iniquity." David was truly sorry for his sin, and God took notice.

God Will Forgive Us Our Sins

Such serious sorrow over sin does not go without reward. It produces forgiveness. The idea of the word *forgiveness* is that of a bookkeeper stamping a bill "Paid in Full." It is the idea of a king declaring a condemned murderer fully pardoned. It is as if a spreadsheet detailing our sins were deleted. Imagine yourself saying, "Lord, do you remember that sin I committed last week?" and God saying, "No, I don't remember it." That is forgiveness.

I know all of that sounds too good to be true, but I am not making this up. Listen to what God promises:

> *"I, even I, am he who blots out your transgressions, for my own sake, and remembers your sins no more."*
>
> Isaiah 43:25

> *"For I will forgive their wickedness and will remember their sins no more."*
>
> Jeremiah 31:34

Late in his life, the mighty hand of God wonderfully healed King Hezekiah. In his prayer of thanks, he said, "You have put all my sins behind your back" (Isaiah 38:17).

In writing of his vision of a better future, the prophet Micah said, "You will again have compassion on us; you will tread our sins underfoot and hurl all our iniquities into the depths of the sea" (Micah 7:19).

God Will Purify Us of All Unrighteousness

God not only cancels our sin. He cleans us up from the inside out. That feels awesome.

In high school, a good friend believed the promise of John 3:16 and trusted Jesus Christ as her Savior. She also acted on the promise of 1 John 1:9 and confessed her sins. When she was telling me about it the next day, I asked her, "How did it feel?"

She gave me a huge smile and said, "Amazing! For the first time since I was a little girl, I felt really, truly clean. . .clean on the inside. I felt like a little girl dancing in the fresh, gentle rain of a spring shower. I have never felt this good before!"

He Loves You

One of my favorite Bible verses is Revelation 1:5. It says, "To Him who loved us and washed us from our sins in His own blood. . ." (NKJV). What I like about this verse is that God loves us *before* He washes us.

When my son Andrew was a toddler, our happy family was out walking by a pond one afternoon. The pond was pretty, but the section we were near happened to be covered with a layer of pea-green scum.

We had stopped by the side of the pond as his older brother, Daniel, threw a rock in the pond. Andrew had to do everything his older brother did, so he picked up a stone. But he was still unsteady on his feet. The force of throwing the stone into the water propelled him into the scum-covered pond, face-first. The pond was shallow around the edges, but he was totally submerged. All that was showing were the bottoms of his tennis shoes, which stuck out through the green scum.

Alarmed, my wife, Cathy, cried, "Dave, get him out!" Being a brave dad, I reached in and pulled him up by his ankles. Andrew, of course, was scared and crying. He also was completely covered in stinky, pea-green pond scum.

Then Cathy called out, "Give him a hug."

I was torn. I desperately love my son. But I absolutely detest reeking pond scum. It gives me the creeps. While I paused to count the cost, Cathy, a true mom, sprang into action. She grabbed him up in both arms and hugged him close.

I felt a bit embarrassed.

Reflecting back on that moment, I was so glad that God loves us before He forgives us and washes us. In fact, His great love is the reason He is willing to forgive us and wash us. That is encouraging!

A *Final Encouragement*

If God could forgive David's big sin, He certainly can forgive you of any sin in your life. You don't have to be perfect or one of the spiritual superelite. You just need to be truly sorry. You need to confess your sin and ask for forgiveness. The Lord will forgive your sins and cleanse your heart. That's God's promise.

11

God's Promise of Godly Confidence

PHILIPPIANS 1:6

Do you lack confidence? What do you do when your faith is wavering? How do you respond when you are faced with a gnawing awareness that your faith is too small? How will you deal with those times when you doubt your ability to make a difference? What do you do when you feel like you can't get through? If you are not sure of how to answer those questions, you are not alone.

Crisis of Faith

A young man named Billy was once at a crisis of faith and confidence. He realized that his wavering faith could not enable him to minister to others effectively. Despairingly, he went out into the woods to pray and think. There he found this promise:

> *Being confident of this, that he who began a good work in you will carry it on to completion until the day of Christ Jesus.*
>
> PHILIPPIANS 1:6

As he read those words, God spoke to his need. Later he wrote, "From that day to this [God] has never stopped giving and performing that which He has begun."[1]

With that promise, Billy was able to launch out as an evangelist. Maybe you have heard of him. His name is Billy Graham, one of the most influential Christians of the twentieth century. He has preached the gospel to more people in live audiences than anyone else in history—over 210 million people in more than 185 countries and territories. Hundreds of millions more have been reached through television, video, film, and webcasts. He has led hundreds of thousands of individuals to Christ, which is the main thrust of his ministry. Dr. Graham has preached in remote African villages and in the heart of New York City. Those to whom he has ministered have ranged from heads of state to the simple-living Aborigines of Australia and the wandering tribes of Africa. Since 1977 Billy has conducted preaching missions in virtually every country of the former Eastern Bloc, including Russia. Mr. Graham has written twenty-four books, many of which have become top sellers.

Wow! Think of it. One little promise rekindled the faith and relaunched the ministry of Billy Graham. Let's go back and look at that Scripture more deeply.

> *Being confident of this, that he who began a good work in you will carry it on to completion until the day of Christ Jesus.*
>
> PHILIPPIANS 1:6

This promise, like the others, has two sides to it—the human and the divine. The human prerequisite is to be confident in God. We are responsible for believing God's Word, trusting God's ability, and having faith in God's timing. This is not easy. We often can't see God's work. Much of His best work is done underground, invisible to the human eye.

Being confident is not always easy. Sometimes it involves great patience. God doesn't work according to our time frame. He does things according to His schedule, not ours. Often He is much more patient than we are. He is content to allow a situation to go on for weeks, months, years, and even decades, seemingly with no divine activity. For example, Joseph spent over a dozen years in slavery and in prison before God's work became evident and Joseph was released to become prime minister of Egypt. But that's nothing. Moses spent forty years in the desert before God showed up to set him on his course for delivering Israel. And then he spent another forty years leading a group of whiny people through the wilderness before they reached the Promised Land.

Confident faith is especially tough when things get worse before they get better. A friend of mine recently remodeled his house. The house was old and worn. The first thing the crew did was tear everything up and make a huge mess. Believe me, the house looked much better *before* the remodeling started. But little by little, progress was made, and eventually it looked better and was structurally stronger.

When my friend showed me the finished product, he said, "The outcome was worth the mess. Several times I wished we had just left things as they were and never even started, but now I am so glad we did not quit on the process."

It is so with us. God goes to work, and things actually look much worse than before. But if we stay with it, we'll be very well pleased with the finished product.

Staying confident can be difficult. But confidence in God to do as He has promised and finish the work He has begun in you is powerful. It releases Him to complete it.

God Promises to Do It

The promise of Philippians 1:6 was written by Paul as he sat in a Roman prison chained to guards 24/7. As he reflected on his life in God and his ministry to others, Paul no doubt realized how often and firmly he had stood on God's promise. From the beginning of his life in Christ, Paul knew that it would be tough. God's plan for Paul was big and difficult. In order to see it become a reality, he would need great faith. As God was calling Paul, this is what God said:

> *"This man is my chosen instrument to carry my name before the Gentiles and their kings and before the people of Israel. I will show him how much he must suffer for my name."*
>
> ACTS 9:15–16

This all came true. Paul brought the gospel to the Israelites. He took the gospel to the Gentiles and shared it with their leaders. He agonized for the sake of the name of Jesus Christ. Now, as he sat suffering in jail, he was on the verge of sharing Jesus with the emperor of the world, Caesar himself.

Inwardly, Paul wrestled with a lack of confidence. Often he asked his friends to pray that he would be bold (Colossians 4:3; Ephesians 6:18–19; 1 Thessalonians 5:25). God responded to these prayers. With powerful boldness, Paul launched his vast ministry and faced persecution and suffering. He fearlessly shared Jesus Christ before angry crowds, indignant judges, and skeptical kings. He confidently gave directions, took risks, and made decisions. He was the picture of confidence.

Paul lived with an abiding, contagious confidence that God would fulfill what He had promised. Summarizing his experience, Paul wrote, "The one who calls you is faithful and he will do it" (1 Thessalonians 5:24).

God Is Able

Too many times I have said, "I am absolutely overwhelmed," or "I am too busy," or "I need more time," or "I don't understand," or "I am so tired."

Unlike me, God has never said any of those words. That's because, unlike any of us, God has no limits. He is eternal and unbounded by time. In fact, He dwells outside the realm of space and time. He is omniscient—all knowing. He is omnipotent—almighty. He has unlimited strength and power. God has all the time, wisdom, and strength to keep His promises. So if He says that He will do something, you'd better believe He is able to carry it out.

Trust Him

Paul did not become so bold through his own strength. Even though he was an extremely intelligent and gifted man, he said that his ministry was not based on his intellect or eloquence but was the result of God's power (1 Corinthians 1:16; 2:1–5). The secret of his great success was that he relied on God.

> *I can do everything through him who gives me strength.*
>
> PHILIPPIANS 4:13

Billy Graham did not become a powerhouse preacher and leader on his own. God did it while Graham trusted. He has testified that from time to time he knew God was providing him with special strength for a certain task. "Sometimes," Dr. Graham said, "as I have lain awake at night the quiet assurance has come that I was being filled with the Spirit for the task that lay ahead."[2]

I Can't. You Can. Please Do.

I have worked hard to develop a life of prayer, but I am not eloquent. Much of my praying is the offering of simple prayers. One simple prayer I find myself saying to God often is this: "I can't. You can. Please do."

That prayer says much more than six words. When I pray it, here is what I am saying to God:

1. "I can't." I acknowledge my inability to meet the challenge. I am not big enough, smart enough, or strong enough to do it. If it is totally up to me, it won't happen.
2. "You can." I am expressing my faith in God. I communicate my confidence in God to be sufficient for the task. I rest on the fact that He is big enough, smart enough, and strong enough for anything at hand.
3. "Please do." I ask Him to act. I expect Him to fulfill His promise.

A *Final Encouragement*

God has begun a good work in you. He is not finished with you yet. He will complete it. He did it for Billy Graham. He did it for Paul. He has done it for countless others, and He will do it for you. Be confident in Him.

Notes

1. Hubert A. Elliot, ed. *Bible Words That Have Helped Me* (New York: Grosset and Dunlop, 1963), 84.
2. Billy Graham, quoted in Elmer Towns, *Understanding the Deeper Life* (Old Tappan, NJ: Revell, 1988), 214–215.

12

God's Promise of Inner Strength

Isaiah 40:28–31

Who says the Bible is dull? How can people generalize that godly people are boring? Anyone who says or thinks that living for God is mundane never met Elijah.

When Elijah blew out of the desert onto the pages of the Scriptures, he stuck his bony prophet's finger in the face of wicked King Ahab and declared that there would be no rain in Israel until he said so (1 Kings 17:1). That was a bold and reckless act. Ahab was notorious for executing prophets for much less brashness than that. However, Elijah not only lived; his word came true. It did not rain in Israel for three years.

Later we read of Elijah's providing a starving widow with daily food through a perpetually replenishing jar of flour and jug of oil (1 Kings 17:7–16). Then, when the widow's son died, Elijah raised him from the dead (1 Kings 17:17–24)!

But those feats were nothing compared to his next display. Imagine one man fearlessly standing alone in a valley in view of hundreds of thousands of people surrounding him on the hillsides. Imagine Elijah facing 850 prophets of the false god Baal. Then picture Elijah challenging them to a public duel to prove which god was the true God, Baal or Jehovah.

See the 850 priests of Baal begin the morning by praying and pleading for Baal, the lightning god, to come down and ignite their sacrifice with fire. Watch as Elijah taunts them. Watch the frustrated pagan prophets continue late into the afternoon shadows, desperately shouting out and cutting themselves before Baal, trying to persuade him to respond. See their efforts meet with nothing but disappointing silence.

Hear the crowd gasp as Elijah brazenly soaks his sacrifice with barrel after barrel of water until the trench around the altar is full. Listen as he simply prays:

> *"O LORD, God of Abraham, Isaac and Israel, let it be known today that you are God in Israel and that I am your servant and have done all these things at your command. Answer me, O LORD, answer me, so these people will know that you, O LORD, are God, and that you are turning their hearts back again."*
>
> 1 KINGS 18:36–37

Stand amazed as a bolt of fire shoots down out of heaven and explodes in the sopping-wet sacrifice. Remain speechless as the wet sacrifice bursts into flames. Watch the flames spread until they have consumed not only the bull but also the wood, the rocks of the altar, and all the water in the trench surrounding the altar. Join the frightened, humbled, excited crowd as you dive on your face, shouting, "The LORD—he is God! The LORD—he is God!" (1 Kings 18:39).

Ordinary Man, Extraordinary Strength

Elijah was an unusual man with rare boldness and incredible spiritual power. Yet the Scriptures remind us that he was just as human as you and me. His amazing strength was not his own. Elijah's outstanding quality was his extraordinary ability to draw his strength and power from God.

> *Elijah was a man just like us. He prayed earnestly that it would not rain, and it did not rain on the land for three and a half years. Again he prayed, and the heavens gave rain, and the earth produced its crops.*
>
> JAMES 5:17–18

The Secret of His Strength

When I study the sketch of Elijah's life recorded in the sacred Scriptures, I find it easy to overlook an event that was the core and foundation of his remarkable strength and power. It occurred right after he predicted the three-year drought and before he performed the miracles with the widow and called down fire on the sacrifice.

> *Then the word of the LORD came to Elijah: "Leave here, turn eastward and hide in the Kerith Ravine, east of the Jordan. You will drink from the brook, and I have ordered the ravens to feed you there." So he did what the LORD had told him. He went to the Kerith Ravine, east of the Jordan, and stayed there.*
>
> 1 KINGS 17:2–5

This tiny vignette reveals why Elijah was able to be so mighty *for* the Lord. He spent time alone *with* the Lord. He hid himself from people in order to nourish himself in the Lord.

Later in his life, when the pressure of fleeing the wrath of Ahab was too intense, Elijah again went into the desert alone and was refreshed (1 Kings 19:3–90). There he met the Lord in an intense and personal way (1 Kings 19:10–18).

Different Man, Same Secret

Jesus is the Son of God. He is fully God, yet He is also fully man. He got hungry and thirsty. He got tired and took naps. When Jesus' ministry began, the load of His daily duties was staggering. On one particular Sabbath, as He was teaching in the synagogue, He was confronted by a demonized man. Jesus cast out the demon (Mark 1:21–27).

Leaving the synagogue with some friends, Jesus went to Peter's house. There Peter's mother-in-law was sick in bed with a fever. Jesus went in and healed her. She got up and helped fix lunch (Mark 1:29–31).

Later that evening the entire town gathered outside the door, gawking as Jesus healed the sick and liberated the demonized. This continued late into the night (Mark 1:32–34).

What an exhausting day!

Any normal man would have been worn out by half as much activity. But the next day, Jesus launched out in a multiple-city preaching and deliverance tour (Mark 1:36–39).

How did He do it? Where did He get His strength? What was his secret?

The Secret of His Strength

Tucked in the middle of this account in Mark's gospel is a golden gem of life-changing insight. Read it carefully:

> *Very early in the morning, while it was still dark, Jesus got up, left the house and went off to a solitary place, where he prayed.*
>
> MARK 1:35

How did Jesus combat the fatigue of a draining day of ministry? The same way we should. He took time away from others so He could trust God in prayer. Notice carefully what He did:

"Very early in the morning, while it was still dark"—Jesus chose a solitary time.

"Jesus got up, left the house"—Jesus distanced Himself from people for a time.

". . .went off to a solitary place"—Jesus chose a solitary place.

". . .where He prayed."

Like Elijah, Jesus found the source of His strength in the Father and the secret of His strength in prayer.

Jesus got away *from* others so He could get away *with* the Father. He sought physical solitude in order to address His spiritual needs. He not only got still before God; He got alone with God. He practiced solitary prayer.

This was Jesus' secret for staying fresh, sharp, full, centered, and on track. During His three-and-a-half years of intense ministry, He practiced waiting on the Father in solitude to keep His spiritual tank full and His emotional battery charged.

Don't we need to learn to do the same? If the Son of God needed to pray, how much more do you and I? If the Son of God rose early and went to a solitary place to pray, shouldn't you and I?"

The sad reality is that most of us are too busy, too crowded, and too cluttered to stay spiritually sharp. Our lives are filled with too much activity, too much noise, and too many relationships, so we have little time for God. Our lives are so full of stuff—good stuff, perhaps, but still stuff—that there is little room for God.[1]

A Promise to Weary People

As we go through life, it is easy to get inwardly worn down. Consistently choosing to do good can empty our emotional reservoir. We also go through rib-rocking blows that can crush us. Without great strength, we can crumble under the weight of it all. It is not that we need more physical strength. We usually need more emotional strength, increased mental toughness, and greater spiritual fortitude. In other words, we need inner strength.

Isaiah is written to people facing tremendous trials: war, famine, persecution, and corruption, to name a few. To such weary people, Isaiah pointed to a wonderful promise:

> *Have you not known? Have you not heard? The everlasting God, the LORD, the Creator of the ends of the earth, neither faints nor is weary. His understanding is unsearchable. He gives power to the weak, and to those who have no might He increases strength. Even the youths shall faint and be weary, and the young men shall utterly fall, but those who wait on the LORD shall renew their strength; they shall mount up with wings like eagles, they shall run and not be weary, they shall walk and not faint.*
>
> ISAIAH 40:28–31 NKJV

This sounds almost too good to be true—renewed strength, wings like those of eagles, strong legs to keep going, and spiritual stamina to not quit. Often that's exactly what we need. The question is, how do we get it? Look again at verse 31: "But those who *wait on the LORD* shall renew their strength."

The Way to Inner Strength Is Waiting on the Lord

The picture is clear. If I do not *wait* on God, I will be *weighted* down by life. What does it mean to wait on the Lord?

1. *Waiting on the Lord means taking time with God.*

Waiting is a time-oriented word. It implies spending a quantity of quality time with the Lord.

The story is told of an American on a trip to Africa many years ago. His entourage hiked for six days. On the seventh day, he awoke the men and was ready to push on. The leader of the men carrying his cargo said, "We will not be going today."

The man was exasperated. Why wouldn't they go? He'd pay them extra. He was in a hurry to get where he was going. They had to press on.

"No," the leader said.

"Why?" the man cried.

"We walked fast and far all week. Today we must wait for our souls to catch up with us."

I have a suspicion that many of us have left our souls back in the dust somewhere. It would not hurt us to slow down and wait for them to catch up. How much time did you spend this week with God? How much unhurried quality time did you spend with the God who can renew your waning strength?

2. *Waiting on the Lord requires trusting Him.*

The word translated "wait" in the above verse can also be translated "hope in." It means "to rely upon." I think we often are tired because we are weighed down from carrying things we have no business carrying. Mentally and emotionally, we carry loads of responsibility that grind us down. We must learn to take on less and trust God with the rest. We need to realize that He is big enough to shoulder the load. We need to trust Him.

Then He'll give us strength.

3. *Waiting on the Lord requires talking it out with God in prayer.*

Both Elijah (James 5:17–18) and Jesus (Mark 1:35) gained renewal and refreshment from the Lord in prayer. Prayer is talking with God. It is telling Him how you feel and what you need.

Prayer is verbally looking at life from God's perspective. It is receiving the relief of seeing the bigger picture and tracing the easily unnoticed hand of the Father.

A Final Encouragement

We need inner strength. What should we do? We should do the same thing Elijah, Jesus, and countless others have done. Live by a promise. The condition for inner strength is waiting on the Lord.

Note

1. For more on solitude in prayer, see Dave Earley, *Prayer Odyssey* (Shippensburg, PA: Destiny Image, 2004), 25–28.

13

God's Promise of Answered Prayer

Matthew 7:7–11

A missionary in the Andes of Ecuador was deathly sick with typhus. His young wife dyed her wedding dress black. His friends purchased a coffin. He was "so far out into the River of Death that [he] was closer to the other side than to this." Utterly incapacitated, he knew he would very soon be in eternity.

At the same time, in faraway New England, believers gathered at a Bible conference. Their study was interrupted by a deep and heavy burden for this very missionary. And so they knelt and prayed with such agony of spirit that they were unaware that mealtime had come and gone. They did not know that the man in Ecuador was delirious and at death's door, that his bride's wedding dress had become a widow's garment. By midafternoon, the burden in their spirits lifted and they had heavenly assurance that their prayers were answered.

That missionary was the late Raymond Edman, president of Wheaton College. He later testified that in those hours as strangers prayed for him, he "experienced a sweet sense of the love of God in Christ such as I had never known before in all the years of my life." After two weeks, he returned to the land of the living.[1]

What amazes me about Dr. Edman's story is the power of the prayers of people thousands of miles away from him. It reminds me of one of the most encouraging promises in the Bible:

"Ask and it will be given to you; seek and you will find; knock and the door will be opened to you. For everyone who asks receives; he who seeks finds; and to him who knocks, the door will be opened. Which of you, if his son asks for bread, will give him a stone? Or if he asks for a fish, will give him a snake? If you, then, though you are evil, know how to give good gifts to your children, how much more will your Father in heaven give good gifts to those who ask him!"

MATTHEW 7:7–11

What do you need? Is it wisdom, strength, food?

What do you need? Do you need guidance, forgiveness, healing, help with a troubled child?

What do you need? Is it money, a job, empowerment to minister, favor with a superior, a promotion?

Do you need a miracle?

God's response to your need is one little word.

Ask.

Ask is a simple word describing a simple act. In its raw sense, it means to use words to express desires. It conveys the concept of recognizing need and seeking the ability of another to meet it. Such an act requires humility.

When used of prayer, *ask* is very much a two-sided word. On one side is our insufficiency, and on the other lies God's all-sufficiency; on one side is our weakness, on the other, God's strength; our dependency rests on one side, and God's dependability on the other. The act of asking is what stretches between the two, connecting them. For us it is a powerful connection. Without it, God's infinite ability to act on our behalf is untapped, wasted, and useless.

By definition, prayer is talking with God. In practice, prayer is asking and receiving. The words used most often for prayer in both the Old and New Testaments mainly mean "ask." In its purest sense, prayer is asking. You have not really prayed until you have asked God for something that is needed.

Someone once said, "God answers prayers in four ways: 'Yes,' 'No,' 'Wait,' and 'You gotta be kidding.' " Someone else said, "If our request is wrong, God says 'No'; if our timing is wrong, God says 'Slow'; if we are wrong, God says 'Grow.' If our request is right, our timing is right, and we are right, God says 'Go!' " But Jesus said, "Ask and it shall be given to you."

Prayer Is Asking

When Jesus taught His disciples to pray, He taught them to ask the Father for things. John R. Rice, the great country evangelist of the first part of the twentieth century, wrote, "Asking is prayer and prayer is asking. So when God invites us to pray, He invites us to ask things of Him."[2]

Have you ever noticed that when people prayed in the Bible, they asked God for things? Notice the short, simple prayers of these people in the Bible:

Listen to Peter out on the Sea of Galilee sinking into the waves after walking on the water with Jesus: "Lord, save me!" (Matthew 14:30).

Pay attention to the blind man: "Jesus, Son of David, have mercy on me!" (Mark 10:47). "Rabbi, I want to see" (Mark 10:51).

Eavesdrop on the prayer of the thief on the cross: "Jesus, remember me when you come into your kingdom" (Luke 23:42).

Hear the heartbroken mother: "Lord, Son of David, have mercy on me! My daughter is suffering terribly from demon-possession"

(Matthew 15:22). "Lord, help me!" (Matthew 15:25).

Think about this: The only prayer Jesus ever held up as errant was one that asked nothing.

> *"Two men went up to the temple to pray, one a Pharisee and the other a tax collector. The Pharisee stood up and prayed about himself: 'God, I thank you that I am not like other men—robbers, evildoers, adulterers—or even like this tax collector. I fast twice a week and give a tenth of all I get.' "*
>
> LUKE 18:10–12

When I first got married and my wife and I went shopping, I began to notice how different men and women could be. For my wife and me, shopping meant two completely different things. She had never had much money, so to her shopping meant "looking." She could look all day. I grew up working a paper route, so I always had some cash but not much time. To me shopping meant "buying"—walking in, seeing what I wanted, buying it, and leaving. The whole process may take ten to fifteen minutes, tops. I figured, if you are not going to buy, why shop?

God has promised that the storehouse of heavenly blessings is opened at the sound of genuine requests. We do not have to merely look. We have the power to ask for exactly what we need. And God wants to give it to us.

If It Is Good to Have, It Is Good to Ask For

I think many of us will get to heaven and find that God wanted to give us so much more, if only we had asked for it. I would rather ask for something and have God refuse than not get it because I failed to ask. If you really want something, and it would not be an embarrassment for God to give it to you, ask.

Anything you have a right to want, you have a right to ask for. Every Christian should take every desire to God in prayer. But if you cannot honestly pray for something, it is a sin to desire it. Ask God to remove a desire if it is wrong. If the desire itself is not wrong, however, then you should ask God to fulfill it![3]

Keep Asking

The verbs in Matthew 7:7, "ask," "seek," and "knock," carry the sense of persistence. Because of the verb tense, you could translate these words in this way: *Keep on* asking, *keep on* seeking, *keep on* knocking. For a variety of reasons, we may not receive what we desire the first time we ask for it. But from Matthew 7:7 and the parable of the persistent widow in Luke 18:1–8, we know that in prayer, persistence pays.

Persistent Prayer Pays

George Mueller modeled persistent prayer. He would pray until he felt he knew God's will about a matter and then keep bringing this to God in prayer until he got his answer. Mueller claimed that he saw over ten thousand immediate answers to prayer. His secret? He asked.

For example, he wrote in his autobiography:

> *In November 1844 I began to pray daily for the conversion of five individuals. I prayed every day without a single intermission. . . . Eighteen months elapsed before the first of the five was converted. I thanked God and prayed on for the others. Five years elapsed, and the second was converted. I thanked God for the second and prayed on*

> *for the other three. Day by day, I continued to pray for them, and six years passed before the third was converted. I thanked God for the three and went on praying for the other two.*
>
> *[I have] been praying day-by-day for thirty-six years for the conversion of these individuals, and yet they remain unconverted. I hope in God, I pray on, and look yet for the answer. They are not converted yet, but they will be.*[4]

He kept praying for these two individuals for a total of fifty-two years. One was saved at Mueller's funeral and the other one a few weeks later!

Once Mueller needed a new orphan house for three hundred needy children. After ninety-three days of asking God to provide land, a landowner called him. The man said he'd been awakened at 3:00 a.m. and couldn't get the idea of selling to Mueller out of his mind. So he wanted to know if Mueller would buy it at about roughly half the price he'd been asking. Next, God provided the money for the land and the building!

A Final Encouragement

If you have a need, your first step should be to seek the Lord in prayer. He will answer if we will ask. That's His promise.

Notes

1. V. Raymond Edman, *They Found the Secret* (Grand Rapids, MI: Zondervan, 1984), 143–146.
2. J. R. Rice, *Prayer: Asking and Receiving* (Chicago: Moody Press, 1961), 130.
3. Ibid.
4. George Mueller, quoted in Basil Miller, *George Muller* (Minneapolis: Bethany Fellowship, 1943), 146.

14

God's Promise of Invincible Love

ROMANS 8:38–39

I am not necessarily a "huggy" person, but there are days when I really need a hug. You know what I mean. Life is not playing fair; things are not turning your way; everything is uphill, harder than you ever expected; deep down inside you wonder if God really loves you.

He does. It's the promise of Romans 8:38–39.

> *For I am convinced that neither death nor life, neither angels nor demons, neither the present nor the future, nor any powers, neither height nor depth, nor anything else in all creation, will be able to separate us from the love of God that is in Christ Jesus our Lord.*
>
> ROMANS 8:38–39

The Desperado

How could anyone not love this promise? It encourages us that God's love is so invincible that it overcomes death, demons, past failures, present problems, future fears, and anything else we could imagine. It tells us that God loves us even if we may not feel like He loves us, if we see ourselves as unlovable, if life seems unfair. The Lord loves us even if He has been silent and our prayers have gone unanswered. God loves us even when everyone else appears to be doing better than we are, when we feel like we have hurt God, when we have run from Him.

Two thousand years ago, Jesus told the story of a desperado who ran away from home only to find out that everything he was desperately looking for was back home with his father. The boy is commonly referred to as the prodigal son.

I love this story because I have been a desperado. My desperado days were those when I desperately tried to run from God, came to my senses, and returned to find His arms still open.

The story of this first-century desperado reminds us of the invincible power of God's love. It shows us that in God's heart, there is always a fire in the fireplace and a place for us at the table.

Running from Love

> *There was a man who had two sons. The younger one said to his father, "Father, give me my share of the estate." So he divided his property between them.*
>
> LUKE 15:11–12

Two unusual things occurred at the very start of this story. First, the younger son asked for his inheritance while his father was still alive and in good health. In that culture, this was an unthinkably selfish act and the ultimate insult to a father. The father would be expected to refuse such a request.

This leads us to the second unusual occurrence. The father divided the inheritance! His dividing of the inheritance would have been public knowledge, and the family would have been shamed before the entire community. This is the first of several times in this story the father goes against tradition. The rest of the story makes it clear that the son's share of the estate was substantial.

Not long after that, the younger son got together all he had, set off for a distant country and there squandered his wealth in wild living.

Luke 15:13

When the younger son got together all he had, he sold his part of the family estate. This would have further shamed the family, because Jewish law did not permit a child to sell his inheritance until after the father died. Yet the self-centered son didn't care.

Then it got worse. The absolute unpardonable sin for a Jewish son was to lose his family's inheritance to non-Jews. In ancient days, if any violator of this law ever came home, villagers would take a large earthenware jar, fill it with burned nuts and corn, and dramatically break it in front of the guilty individual. While doing this the people would shout, "This man is now cut off from his people!" From that point on, no one in the village would have any contact with the offender. Yet the desperado did not care. He persisted in partying all his money away.

Ruining His Life

After he had spent everything, there was a severe famine in that whole country, and he began to be in need.

Luke 15:14

Normally a son in need would simply return home. This desperado had burned his bridges and so closed the door on a return. He had publicly disgraced his father and family. He couldn't return now, after losing his money to non-Jewish people in a far country. The first villagers to see him would call for the excommunication ceremony, and he would be publicly cut off from his people. Therefore, the desperado came up with a plan.

> *So he went and hired himself out to a citizen of that country, who sent him to his fields to feed pigs. He longed to fill his stomach with the pods that the pigs were eating, but no one gave him anything.*
>
> LUKE 15:15–16

To come home, he had to earn the money back. Yet as a pig herder, he received a place to sleep but no money. So he was in a hopeless situation.

Returning Home to the Father's Love

> *When he came to his senses, he said, "How many of my father's hired men have food to spare, and here I am starving to death! I will set out and go back to my father and say to him: Father, I have sinned against heaven and against you. I am no longer worthy to be called your son; make me like one of your hired men." So he got up and went to his father.*
>
> LUKE 15:17–20

This entire story shows the desperado doing dumb things. Then he finally did something smart. He returned home.

He came to his senses. "Aha! Eating good food with the guys who work at my dad's farm is better than eating pig slop. Being around a family is better than being alone. Being close to my father is better than being far away. It would be better to be a hired servant at home than a free man far away."

He remembered that life was always better at his father's house. And for us, life is always better with our heavenly Father. There is no guilt, no shame, and no emptiness in the Father's house. There is belonging and acceptance, dignity and destiny. There is mercy, grace, truth, meaning, fulfillment, and forgiveness in the Father's house. Invincible love reigns in the Father's house.

Receiving the Father's Invincible Love

> *But while he was still a long way off, his father saw him and was filled with compassion for him; he ran to his son, threw his arms around him and kissed him.*
>
> LUKE 15:20

The son deserved the ceremony of rejection. Instead, he was given an undeserved, warm reception. The father's four loving actions blow my mind!

First, the father saw his son. The fact that the father saw the son implies that the father was on the lookout for the son. The son was gone a long time, yet throughout that period the father kept looking for the son to return. The father never gave up.

Wow! It reminds me that our heavenly Father does not quit on us. He is patiently watching and awaiting our return.

Second, the father felt compassion for his son. He was not filled with hurt. He was not filled with wounded pride. He was filled with love.

It is the same with our heavenly Father. He does not view us through the distorted lens of a bruised ego. He is full of love for us.

Third, the father ran to his son. If the father saw him first, he had every right to call for the ceremony of rejection. After all, he was the one who had been disgraced. Or if he did not call for the ceremony of rejection, he could have seen the son, made sure the son saw him, turned his back, and let another family member be the first to speak to the son. But he did not.

I am so glad that my heavenly Father does not hold back. Often in the past God has pursued me, and still He pursues me on my desperado days.

Fourth, the father hugged and kissed his son. No folded arms. No stiff handshake. No questions. No words of anger, frustration, or rebuke. Just a simple, big, deep, heartfelt hug.

There is nothing like that unmistakable, indescribable, supernatural sense of being drawn back into the arms of the heavenly Father. Nothing compares with the warm favor of His renewed affection.

The Restoring Power of Love

> *The son said to him, "Father, I have sinned against heaven and against you. I am no longer worthy to be called your son." But the father said to his servants, "Quick! Bring the best robe and put it on him. Put a ring on his finger and sandals on his feet. Bring the fattened calf and kill it. Let's have a feast and celebrate. For this son of mine was dead and is alive again; he was lost and is found." So they began to celebrate.*
>
> Luke 15:21–24

The son deserved the ceremony of rejection. The father had every right to hoist a jar of burnt nuts and corn high over his head and then smash it dramatically in the desperado's face.

But the father did not disown him or make him a servant. He restored him as his son! He gave him an elaborate and expensive party! He presented to him the best robe. He put a ring on his finger. He invited a big crowd of people and served a fatted calf (it would take a lot of people a long time to eat a fatted calf). The father gave his wayward son a big-time celebration. This is a picture of powerful, invincible love!

Twenty-First-Century Desperados

Every word of this story is a portrait of God's invincible love for desperados. Make no mistake about it. We are all desperados, desperately seeking love as we wrestle with loneliness, hopelessness, frustration, and emptiness. We all seek a love that provides us with genuine acceptance, lasting hope, deep meaning, and ultimate destiny. Each of us thirsts for a truly triumphant love that will reach through our pride and rebellion to love us.

Such an invincible love is available. God, our Father, has promised it to us. But like the first-century desperado, we twenty-first-century desperados must come to our senses, stop running from the Father, and hurry home to His outstretched arms. He is waiting.

A *Final Encouragement*

You can never run so far that you can't get back home. The Father is watching and waiting for you to return. He won't scold or condemn. He will forgive and restore. He'll even throw a party. But you have to run home.

15

God's Promise of Timely Promotion

Psalm 75:6–7

Does your heart ever burn for a higher status in life? Do you live with a gnawing sense that you're meant for more? Maybe you, like me, long for a greater position of influence in order to touch more people for God. Maybe you are worn out from dreaming and scheming of how to get there. God has a promise for you, but first a story.

Bad News for the Jews

Esther was an extremely beautiful young Jewish woman. Her cousin, Mordecai, was a very good and noble man. However, the king's highest official, Haman, was a viciously evil man with more power than he could handle. Nearly twenty-five hundred years ago in the land of Persia, their three lives were woven together to tell a fascinating story of God's principles of promotion.

One day the Persian king Xerxes ordered all of his servants to bow down before Haman in order to honor him. But a Jewish man named Mordecai refused. He would only bow before the true God, and Haman did not qualify. When he discovered Mordecai's unwillingness to bow down to him, Haman hatched a plot.

"Why kill one Jew when I can annihilate them all?" he reasoned. So he offered to pay the bill for the extinction of the Jews throughout Xerxes' vast kingdom, which ranged from

India to Ethiopia. He reasoned that by plundering the Jews he could collect the millions of dollars it would take to kill them. Haman presented a prejudiced case against the Jews to the king and obtained Xerxes' permission to carry out his plan.

The Divinely Positioned Person of Influence

Not long before this, the king had become disillusioned with his wife and wanted a new one. So a special beauty contest was held to find the king a new queen. Esther was selected for the contest. The king fell deeply in love with her and made her the next queen. No one in the palace knew that Esther was a Jew or that Mordecai was her relative. Of course, all of this was according to God's sovereign plan.

When Mordecai heard that Haman was planning to wipe out the Jews, he went to Esther seeking her help. In those days, even a queen was forbidden to approach the king uninvited. To do so could mean death. So Esther asked Mordecai to call all of the Jews to fast on her behalf before she approached the king.

Their fasting made a difference. When Esther entered King Xerxes' presence, he was so happy to see her that he blurted out that he'd gladly give her anything she wanted. But Esther had more than just a pretty face and a shapely figure. She was wise and patient. So she invited the king to return the next night with Haman for a special banquet.

The king so enjoyed the meal that he again offered to give Esther anything she wanted. But she knew that he was not yet ready to grant her huge request. So she again invited Xerxes and Haman to return the next night for another magnificent feast.

After the feast, Haman went home full of himself. He had been invited to eat two meals in a row with the king and queen. Heady with power and angered over Mordecai's seeming disrespect, he ordered the building of a gallows. The next day he planned to ask the king to authorize the execution of the Jew Mordecai.

Timely Bedtime Reading

Back at the palace, God's sovereign plan continued. The king was restless and unable to fall asleep. He ordered the record of the daily events of his palace read to him. The reader read of an event involving Mordecai the Jew. It seemed that some time earlier Mordecai had uncovered a plot to assassinate the king. As a result, the king's life was spared, but Mordecai had somehow gone unrewarded. The king wondered what should be done to honor this unsung hero.

Bad Timing by Haman

As the sun rose over Persia, Haman boldly knocked on the king's door. He hoped to receive permission to execute his nemesis, the faithful Jew Mordecai. But the king had another plan for Mordecai.

King Xerxes brought Haman in and asked him what he suggested should be done for someone the king would like to honor. Haman arrogantly assumed the king was referring to him, so he gushed that the man should be given one of the king's robes, placed on one of the king's horses, and led through the city square, proclaimed as a hero.

The king loved the idea. So he ordered Haman to do this for Mordecai the Jew! Haman had to watch as the man he was hoping to execute was given one of the king's robes, placed on the king's horse, and recognized as a hero!

Don't you love the divine irony?

Haman's Horrible Day

When Mordecai returned from his victory lap, the palace aides arrived to take Haman to dinner. But by then he was losing his appetite.

Unlike Haman, the king greatly enjoyed the meal and once again told Esther that he'd gladly give her anything she asked. Buoyed by her faith in God and driven by the dire situation awaiting her and her people, Esther humbly yet boldly made her request:

> *"If I have found favor with you, O king, and if it pleases your majesty, grant me my life—this is my petition. And spare my people—this is my request. For I and my people have been sold for destruction and slaughter and annihilation. If we had merely been sold as male and female slaves, I would have kept quiet, because no such distress would justify disturbing the king."*
>
> Esther 7:3–4

Then she must have held her breath. But instead of being angry with her, the king was livid against her adversary. He demanded to know the name of the wicked fool who wanted to kill her and her people. To Haman's horror, she was only too happy to oblige the king's request and said, "The adversary and enemy is this vile Haman" (Esther 7:6).

Furious, the king stomped out. Ironically, pathetically, and almost comically, Haman begged Esther for his life. This was a poor choice and bad timing on Haman's part.

Just as the king returned from the palace garden to the banquet hall, Haman was groveling at the couch where Esther was reclining—a bad decision.

The king exclaimed, "Will he even molest the queen while she is with me in the house?" As soon as the word left the king's mouth, they covered Haman's face. Then Harbona, one of the eunuchs attending the king, said, "A gallows seventy-five feet high stands by Haman's house. He had it made for Mordecai, who spoke up to help the king." The king said, "Hang him on it!" So they hanged Haman on the gallows he had prepared for Mordecai. Then the king's fury subsided.

ESTHER 7:8–10

And They Lived Happily Ever After

These were incredible happenings. Instead of killing all the Jews starting with Mordecai, Haman was forced to honor Mordecai. Then Haman was executed on the very gallows he had built to kill Mordecai!

What happened next would have been utterly impossible a few days earlier. Instead of being killed for her brashness, Esther was given her own palace, which just so happened to be Haman's former estate!

On top of that, she was given the power to spare the Jews. Plus, her people were given the authority to kill those who had persecuted them and to confiscate their property. As a result, many non-Jews decided to become Jews!

But the divine icing on the cake is reserved for Mordecai. Instead of being the first Jew killed, he was promoted to Haman's position as the king's highest-ranking official. Wow!

Yay, God!

Esther is the only book of the Bible that does not mention God, although its story has God's fingerprints all over it.

Who else but God led Mordecai to uncover the plot to kill the king? Obviously, the Lord was the One who allowed Esther to become the queen. God kept the king awake that night. The Lord directed the royal reader to expound the account of Mordecai's valor and point out that it had gone unrewarded. God gave Esther favor with the king so he'd grant her every request. And God arranged to bless Esther, spare the Jews, destroy their enemies, and take evil Haman down while lifting honorable Mordecai up.

Yay, God!

Promotion by Preparation and Providence

> *No one from the east or the west or from the desert can exalt a man. But it is God who judges: He brings one down, he exalts another.*
>
> Psalm 75:6–7

Human nature dreams and schemes for promotion, thinking it comes as the result of luck or knowing the right people. But for God's people, promotion is the result of preparation and providence. When all is said and done, God gives the demotions and promotions according to His purpose and plan. He is the ultimate ruler over the universe. Just ask Esther, Mordecai, and Haman. They teach us several lessons about divine promotion.

- *Promotion Ultimately Comes from God*

Ultimately, Mordecai's promotion came from the Lord, not from the king. This was not the only time God gave supernatural promotions in a single day. God exalted Joseph from prisoner to prime minister in a day. God promoted David from shepherd boy to military hero in a day. God lifted Daniel from the ranks of plebe on probation to a position in the king's cabinet in a day.

- *Promotion Comes according to God's Timing, Not Ours*

No doubt, Mordecai would have loved to receive his promotion at the time he uncovered the assassination plot against the king. But if he had been promoted then, Haman would have been his boss and would have been able to hold him back or kill him. However, because the promotion came according to God's timing, it was to a higher position and a better situation. Certainly, God's ways and God's timing are best.

- *Promotion Is Given to Those the Lord Deems Promotable*

Before his promotion, Mordecai was viewed as a good and honorable man. He already held a position in the king's court. He proved himself to be loyal to the king. He was definitely loyal to his people. He refused to worship anyone other than the Lord. He was obviously a man with strong character and good capabilities. And God knew it. Clearly, Mordecai was prepared and ready.

A Twenty-First-Century Promotion

The atmosphere at work was tense on a good day, downright fearful on the others. Dread hung like a black cloud since the company had been bought out. Rumor had it that seventy-five of the staff would be let go.

Debbie had labored under a miserable, vulgar, ungodly woman for three years. Maybe being laid off wouldn't be so bad, at least for a while. But Debbie was a single mom with two teenage daughters, and she desperately needed the income. Her boss hated everything about Debbie's Christianity. She mocked Debbie's ever-positive attitude, disliked her unwillingness to lie, and was very jealous of Debbie's relationship with her daughters. Everyone knew that Debbie would be the first her boss would release if given the opportunity.

The situation cleared some when word was sent down that only 25 percent of the total workforce would be let go. Unfortunately, everyone in Debbie's department was to be released or reassigned.

Debbie was enjoying her day because her boss wasn't around. Everyone assumed she was out sick. Then Debbie's phone rang. She gulped when the vice president's secretary requested that she come up to his office right away. She had always respected the vice president, because he was known around the company as a man of strong ethics and genuine concern for those who worked most closely with him. The other people working in her department avoided making eye contact with her as she made her way to the elevator. Cautiously she sat down in the vice president's office.

He entered briskly through the side door and sat down. "Let's not beat around the bush here," he said. "Your department is being phased-out, and most of the people are being let go, including your boss. But I have received permission to keep the best and the brightest, and that's you. I have been watching you, and you have what it takes. My assistant is retiring at the end of the month, and I want you to take her place. It will mean more responsibility, but. . ." He paused, looking at a paper. Then he smiled and said, "But you'll get a 10 percent raise immediately and a 5 percent increase at the end of the year. What do you think?"

A Final Encouragement

Often we want to get ahead of God's timing. Often we want things to follow our plans. But the Father knows best. It is more productive to focus on being better prepared than to scheme how to get a better job.

When God knows you are ready, when His timing is right, and when it will best advance His purposes, then your promotion will come.

16

God's Promise of Comfort for the Brokenhearted

Psalm 34:18

Betrayed, forsaken, misunderstood, cheated, exhausted, confused. If you have ever wrestled with such feelings and the heartbreaking emotions they bring, you are not alone. King David felt them all at the same time, on a major scale. Though he was forced to flee, he couldn't run from his problems.

Man on the Run

Sneaking through the wilderness, David was a fugitive in the biggest manhunt in the history of Israel. Imagine the thoughts that must have flooded his mind every time he stopped to catch his breath:

> *How did this happen to me? What did I do to deserve this? When will I wake up and find this nightmare over? One day I was anointed the new king. The next thing I knew, I'd killed Goliath. God had used me to save the nation. Immediately, I became the general of the king's army, the husband of the king's daughter, and the darling of the king's people. I was loyal, faithful, successful, secure, and happy.*
>
> *Then—wham!—he king went crazy with jealousy and tried to kill me. He declared me an outlaw and led his*

army out after me. I had to leave my wife, my career, my friends, my reputation, and all I have ever loved to run for my life.

I tried to hide in the last place he'd think of looking for me with the Philistines. But they were still very upset about the Goliath incident, so I had to grovel and slobber and act like a deranged lunatic to escape.

Now King Saul has jumped off the cliff of sanity and gone violently berserk. He murdered eighty-five priests in cold blood just because they had helped me. Saul and his soldiers will not rest until he's cut off my head and fed my carcass to the birds. They are out there, coming after me. What is going on? What did I do wrong? Why is this happening to me? When will this nightmare end?

The Antidote for an Achy-Breaky Heart

Unexpected, undeserved, unexplainable adversity—it happens to all of us, and David found himself neck deep in it. It broke his heart.

David found that nothing hurts as profoundly as a broken heart. It steals our strength, robs our joy, and takes away our peace. It keeps us awake through the night and exhausted through the day.

Yet just as David knew the agony of a crushed spirit, somewhere in that lonely desert he also experienced the universal antidote in a marvelous little promise. Fortunately, he wrote it down in his journal. This three-thousand-year-old promise still holds true today:

The LORD is close to the brokenhearted and saves those who are crushed in spirit.

PSALM 34:18

This promise opens with these key words: "The LORD." He is the prescription for a broken heart. When we ache in inner agony, what we desperately need are love, light, joy, peace, and perspective. God is the source of these and more. Like rays of light and heat that radiate from the sun, God brings health and healing to our aching hurts and deflated spirits. Everything our hurting hearts need flows from the heart of God.

This brings us back to David. He was called a "man after God's own heart" because he learned how to beat a path to God when his spirit was crushed. The psalm in which this promise is found is a four-part primer on the art and science of getting to God when you have a broken heart.

- *Turn Your Pain into Praise*

I will extol the LORD at all times; his praise will always be on my lips. My soul will boast in the LORD; let the afflicted hear and rejoice. Glorify the LORD with me; let us exalt his name together.

PSALM 34:1–3

It seems like an outrageous impossibility—praising God when your heart is broken. But it is very possible. And it does make a huge difference. David determined that God was worthy of praise no matter what. He decided that he would live a life of praise regardless of his circumstances. He practiced praise when times were good, so it was less difficult to praise when all went awry. He turned his pain into praise and found a path to God. Many others have done the same.

Job's heart was pounded and pulverized even more severely than David's was. In one awful day he was stripped of his wealth, ness, career, and employees. Then he was told that all of his children were dead. I cannot imagine the immense weight of grief that crushed his soul. Such pressing sorrow could have driven a normal man to insanity. But Job knew the path to God. He acknowledged his burden and then turned his pain into praise.

> *At this, Job got up and tore his robe and shaved his head. Then he fell to the ground in worship and said: "Naked I came from my mother's womb, and naked I will depart. The LORD gave and the LORD has taken away; may the name of the LORD be praised."*
>
> JOB 1:20–21

Paul and Silas were serving God with everything they had. They were trying to capture Philippi for Christ. But the powers in Philippi captured them, beat them, and threw them into prison. This would have disillusioned and discouraged most people, but not Paul and Silas. They knew the path to God. They turned their pain into praise.

> *About midnight Paul and Silas were praying and singing hymns to God, and the other prisoners were listening to them.*
>
> ACTS 16:25

In the case of Paul and Silas, their praise not only brought them to God but brought God to them in a big way.

> *Suddenly there was such a violent earthquake that the foundations of the prison were shaken. At once all the prison doors flew open, and everybody's chains came loose.*
>
> ACTS 16:26

God sent an earthquake to His imprisoned praisers. You may know the rest of the story. The jailer and his family were saved (Acts 16:31), and Paul and Silas were set free (16:35). Never underestimate the power of praise and thanksgiving. It is the path to God and the prescription for a broken heart.

- *Make Your Grief a Motive for Prayer*

David not only blessed God when life was cursing him; he also turned his problems into prayer, and God answered.

> *I sought the* LORD*, and he answered me; he delivered me from all my fears. Those who look to him are radiant; their faces are never covered with shame. This poor man called, and the* LORD *heard him; he saved him out of all his troubles. The angel of the* LORD *encamps around those who fear him, and he delivers them.*
>
> PSALM 34:4–7

It is important to notice that David did not say that his prayers kept him from experiencing trouble. He said that his prayers saved him out of his troubles. The bad news is that as long as we are on this planet, we will experience heartbreaking trouble. The good news is that prayer allows God to deliver us out of it.

We may feel as though our hearts are so heavy or so angry that we cannot pray. But it is at these times we must pray. We must choose to make the effort to talk with the One who can make things better.

- *Pursue God Even When It Hurts*

What sets David apart from so many others is that His

fervent passion for God was undaunted by the fierce problems he faced. He allowed his difficulties to drive him to God, not away from God. Provision and inner healing were the result.

> *Taste and see that the* LORD *is good; blessed is the man who takes refuge in him. Fear the* LORD, *you his saints, for those who fear him lack nothing. The lions may grow weak and hungry, but those who seek the* LORD *lack no good thing.*
>
> PSALM 34:8–10

Periods of intense, piercing pain are defining moments for the followers of God. They can either force us far from God or draw us amazingly close to Him. It is up to us. If we let our difficulties drive us from God, our heartache will only grow. But if we decide to let our pain press us toward God, we will find a level of soul satisfaction previously unattained and unimagined.

• *Practice Good Living and God-Centered Choices*

When my heart is broken, it pulls my focus off God and onto me. I forget that life is ultimately all about Him, and I begin to live as though it's all about me. I see and hear everything around me through the skewed lens of me. Such a distorted outlook leads to hurt feelings and bad decisions and only makes me more miserable.

Also, when my heart is broken, the enemy loves to whisper through the cracks and tempt me to sin. He will tell me that God failed me and I have an excuse for sin. My old nature gladly accepts any reason to get relief or distraction from the pain. Yet toleration of sin only leads to guilt, and guilt does not heal the brokenhearted. David understood this. Hence, he stepped up his commitment to practice righteous living and make God-centered choices.

> *Come, my children, listen to me; I will teach you the fear of the* LORD. *Whoever of you loves life and desires to see many good days, keep your tongue from evil and your lips from speaking lies. Turn from evil and do good; seek peace and pursue it. The eyes of the* LORD *are on the righteous and his ears are attentive to their cry; the face of the* LORD *is against those who do evil, to cut off the memory of them from the earth. The righteous cry out, and the* LORD *hears them; he delivers them from all their troubles.*
>
> PSALM 34:11–17

A Final Encouragement

> *He heals the brokenhearted and binds up their wounds.*
>
> PSALM 147:3

God has the ability and desire to heal broken hearts. He did it for David, and He has done it for countless others. He can do it for you. Do your part to get to Him, and He'll do His part to mend your heart.

17

God's Promise of Maturity through Adversity

JAMES 1:2–4

He knew adversity. His brother had been illegally arrested, unjustly tried, and violently executed. Now everyone close to him was in jeopardy.

James, the son of Joseph and Mary, the half brother of Jesus, went from skeptic to believer after seeing his brother Jesus resurrected from the dead. At that moment, James's half brother became his Lord and his God. At that moment, Jesus' enemies became James's enemies. He and the others who followed Jesus became targets of persecution.

James began to care for Jesus' followers as a shepherd cares for sheep. All the believers who lived in Jerusalem looked to him for special spiritual care and leadership. The Romans and the Jews focused their abuse on Christians. The Romans taxed them mercilessly and treated them as glorified slaves. The Jews booted them from their families, fired them from their jobs, and accused them of heresy. Soon, Jews and Romans joined forces to throw the Jerusalem Christians in jail and kill their leaders.

The ferocity of the persecution that James' spiritual flock faced was so intense that many fled for their lives and scattered all over the earth. James must have been heartbroken. Beyond that, he saw many of his colleagues imprisoned and killed.

Out of his suffering and sorrow, James penned a powerful

letter to his scattered sheep. In it he gave them one of the most encouraging promises in the Bible:

> *Consider it pure joy, my brothers, whenever you face trials of many kinds, because you know that the testing of your faith develops perseverance. Perseverance must finish its work so that you may be mature and complete, not lacking anything.*
>
> James 1:2–4

These sentences are two sticks of dynamite packed with encouragement. In them, God promises to develop our maturity through adversity. This is very important, because the Lord does not promise to exempt us from adversity.

Some of us struggle because we have the mistaken notion that if God really loved us, He would protect us from problems. This is simply not true. It is *because* God loves us that He allows us to experience adversity. He allows our trials because they produce growth and maturity. The loving God values our growth more than our comfort. He allows our discomfort with good cause.

Many believers accept the myth that Christians don't have problems. Ridiculous! When James records God's promise of maturity through adversity, he is addressing Christians, saying, "my brothers." Many of these people were experiencing problems only because they were Christians. They were forced to abandon their jobs, flee their homes, and run for their lives because they had identified themselves as followers of Jesus.

Sometimes I need to remind myself that I am not home yet. Heaven will be perfect, but I am not there. So I should not be surprised by problems. I should expect them.

Bad Things Do Happen to Good People

Far too often, I catch myself thinking, "Why is this trouble happening to me? I am living for God and doing all the good I can. I live right, so why I am experiencing wrong?" The truth is, bad things happen to good people.

Again I say, some would have us believe that so-called spiritual Christians never face adversity. Absurd! In the first century, the higher someone was positioned in spiritual leadership, the greater the persecution they faced. Godly people face adversity. They always have and always will. Remember, most of the apostles died as martyrs.

Walk through the Bible with me and note the adversity God's people endured. Adam and Eve had a rebellious, murderous son. Sarah was barren until she was ninety years old. Then she had to chase a toddler around!

Job lost his sheep, cattle, oxen, servants, children, and health. Joseph went through slavery and prison. Moses had to deal with Pharaoh, and then he had to lead some of history's all-time greatest whiners. Joshua faced one battle after another. Hannah was barren and had to deal with a cruel adversary.

David was totally innocent, yet he was nearly murdered twice and had to run for his life like a fugitive. Daniel faced a den of hungry lions. Shadrach, Meshach, and Abednego were thrown into a flaming furnace.

Mary watched her son be executed unjustly. Paul was repeatedly beaten and thrown into jail. And James died as a martyr.

Problems are a universal reality of life on this groaning planet—even for Christians!

Choose Joy

Consider it pure joy. . .

James 1:2

A quick study of this opening line of the promise brings several insights. The promise begins with the command, "Consider it pure joy, my brothers, whenever you face trials of many kinds." The fact that this is a command means that we have the option of obeying it or not. It is our choice. This is powerful. We do not have to live as the helpless victims of our circumstances. We can be victors. It is our choice.

Victor, Not Victim

Victor Frankl was a true victor in the midst of awful adversity. He was a Jew in Nazi Germany during World War II and was thrown into the Auschwitz prison camp. Conditions there were unbearable. He experienced extreme suffering from hunger, cold, and brutality. He lived under the threat of imminent extermination. His father, mother, brother, and wife had died in concentration camps. His every possession was lost, every valuable destroyed. Such losses broke most men, and they gave up and died. But Frankl survived, even thrived, and came to understand something we all should know:

> *Everything can be taken from a man but. . .the last of the human freedoms—to choose one's attitude in any given set of circumstances, to choose one's own way.*[1]

We don't have to be victims. Like Victor Frankl, we can be victors. It is our choice.

Problems Produce Perseverance

The testing of your faith develops perseverance.

JAMES 1:3

This promise gives us good reason to choose joy in the midst of adversity. The reason is that adversity produces maturity. Look again at the promise. "Consider it pure joy, my brothers, whenever you face trials of many kinds, *because* you know that the testing of your faith develops perseverance" (emphasis added).

Perseverance is an awesome word that is overlooked and underused in today's vernacular. Don't take it lightly. It is the ability to press through adversity until you come out on the other side.

Run through the Pain

When I was a student, I ran track. My legs were (and still are) short, and I was (and still am) not very fast. But I wanted to earn a varsity letter. So I ran the least popular races. These happened to be the longest races. In the eighth grade, the longest race available was the mile. So that became my specialty, even though I was not all that special.

One day, at the end of a hard practice, the coach asked several of my teammates and me to run a mile race. We were tired, but we agreed.

Somewhere around the three-quarter-mile mark, I hit the wall. My legs turned to lead. My lungs burned. A sharp cramp dug into my rib cage. The finish line appeared to be miles away. The track seemed to be going uphill. Everything inside cried out, "Stop. Lay down. This is too much. You cannot go on."

Then I heard my coach's voice ringing through the air.

"Run *through* the pain," he yelled. "You can do it Earley.

Run *through* the pain."

So I did. His encouragement was what I needed. I found reserves I did not realize I had. As a result, I turned in a better time than anyone expected. I also learned that I could do more than I realized.

Too often when adversity hits, we feel tired and weary. We run *to* the pain. But then we want to quit. God promises to give us what we need to run *through* the pain. He gives us the grace to persevere.

You may have hit a wall of pain in the race of your life. Let me encourage you not to quit. Run through the pain.

No Pain, No Gain

> *Perseverance must finish its work so that you may be mature and complete, not lacking anything.*
>
> JAMES 1:4

I also participated in wrestling. Part of wrestling conditioning is weight lifting. I will never forget my first day in the weight room. I was a skinny ninety-eight-pound freshman surrounded by a horde of mammoth football players. I had lifted weights a little at home, but somehow the weights seemed much heavier in the weight room with everyone watching. I was so sore the next day I could hardly move.

There was a sign on the wall of the weight room that I have never forgotten. Its words are the essence of James 1:4. It said, "No pain. No gain."

I learned the truth of this message. If you lift until your muscles begin to ache and then stop, you will make little or no progress. But lifting through the pain is what makes your muscles grow. Pain produces gain.

Trials can be troubling and terribly painful. Remember, the pain is a tool that produces gain in the development of our character and our spiritual maturity.

Perseverance Produces Maturity

I have three boys, all teenagers. All of them are fully capable of walking on their own and have been since they were a little over a year old. When each boy was about a year old, he took his first steps. After that first staggering attempt to walk, he crashed mightily and cried.

My wife and I had a choice. We could have said, "We love this cute little boy so much that we don't want him to get hurt anymore. From now on one of us will carry him around on a golden pillow. No more painful falling down for our precious little boy."

Today all of our sons are the same size as I am and bigger than their mom. To carry them around on a golden pillow would be impossible. Plus, they would resent us for never allowing them to learn to walk. Such protection would have kept them from maturing.

Instead of pursuing the shortsighted scheme of protecting them from pain, we let them go through it. We let them try to learn to walk. Every time they fell, we'd pick them up, wipe away their tears, and let them go at it again. And they did.

God treats us the same way. His goal is to develop our maturity more than to cater to our comfort. So He allows us to experience adversity and encourages us to press through it. By doing so, we mature.

A Final Encouragement

You will face adversity. As you choose joy in the midst of your adversity and persevere through it, God promises to give you maturity. Don't quit. Run through the pain, and you will grow. That is His promise.

Note

1. Victor Frankl, quoted in Jone Johnson Lewis, "Attitude Quotes" from *Wisdom Quotes: Quotations to Inspire and Challenge,* http://www.wisdomquotes.com/cat_attitude.html (August 25, 2005).

18

God's Promise of Peace Instead of Worry

PHILIPPIANS 4:6–7

Are you a worrier? Do troubling thoughts about what could happen drive you to distraction? Are you skilled at focusing on what could go wrong? Do uncertain situations make you anxious? I understand. Being a worrier at heart, I am always impressed with people who win over worry in the worst situations.

Paul lived a life of victory over anxiety. As an elderly man, he was taken to Rome and held in strict custody in the Praetorium, that is, the barracks of the Praetorian guards attached to the palace of Nero in Rome (Philippians 1:13; 4:22).[1] There he spent two years chained to Roman guards (Philippians 1:12).[2]

If that was not enough to make a man worry, Paul faced probable execution at the hands of the maniacal emperor, Nero, and his newly installed prefect, Tigellinus, whom history calls "a monster in wickedness."[3] Paul's letter, although radiating joy and peace, also reveals his awareness of the possibility of his execution (Philippians 2:17; 3:11).

If I had been in his situation, I would have been tempted to whine and worry. Thoughts of "This is not fair," "Why did this happen to me?" and "What is going to happen next?" would have flooded my mind. But these were not Paul's thoughts. When he sat down to write a letter to his friends at Philippi, not a whiff of worry, fear, or self-pity slipped out. Amazingly, the tone is so worry-free and optimistic that his letter to the

Philippians is often called the "Epistle of Joy"!

Where did Paul get this ability to be at peace in the midst of prison? How could he manifest such joy from jail? What was his secret? How did he do it?

Fortunately for us, Paul did not keep his path to peace to himself. When he penned his letter to the Philippians, he shared the following promise:

> *Do not be anxious about anything, but in everything, by prayer and petition, with thanksgiving, present your requests to God. And the peace of God, which transcends all understanding, will guard your hearts and your minds in Christ Jesus.*
>
> PHILIPPIANS 4:6–7

It is a privilege to possess more than one spiritual gift. I have always joked that as a pastor my two greatest gifts are delegation and irritation. But I have to confess that I also possess the non-spiritual gift of "tending toward anxiety." I am highly analytical. When I cannot figure out how something will work out, I struggle to find peace with it. Unresolved situations and uncertain circumstances drive me to distraction. Once anxious thoughts start running through my mind, it is as though a dam has broken and apprehension flows in such torrents that I struggle mightily to make them stop.

Therefore, I am eternally grateful for the promise of Philippians 4:6–7. It worked for Paul, it works for me, and it will work for you. Let's examine it more closely.

Do Not Worry about Anything

Paul opened the promise with a strong, inclusive directive: "Do not be anxious about anything." Peace won't flow when anxiety clogs the pipe. Worry must be recognized and refused. Anxiety must be flushed out before peace can run freely through the pipes of our minds and souls.

If you are like me, you ask, "How can I stop being anxious? It feels like an involuntary emotion. What is strong enough to turn it off and flush it out?" The answer is found in the next part of the promise.

Pray about Everything

"Do not be anxious about anything, but in everything, by prayer and petition, with thanksgiving, present your requests to God." Notice the last phrase of the above sentence. The only way to stop negative emotions is to replace them with positive actions. The only way to stop greed is to trade it for generosity. The only way to stop bitterness is to substitute forgiveness and love. The only way to defeat fear is to exchange it with faith. And the only way to win over worry is to replace it with grateful prayer. Let's look a little more deeply at exactly how to replace worry with thankful prayer.

Stay Focused on God

Worry has a way of dominating our focus. This is dangerous, because once we become focused on worry, our worries seem to get steadily larger and more complex. In order to defeat anxiety, we must stay fixed on God. He needs to be foremost in our thinking, primary in our conversations, and central in our deeds. As we concentrate on God, we will see Him for who He is—the One who is bigger than anything we could worry about.

Turn Pressures into Prayers

The term *petition* speaks of "making specific requests to God." Just as we are tempted to worry over specific problems, we need to practice definite petitioning in prayer.

To keep from being eaten by anxiety, I have learned that I must turn my pressures into prayers. Every morning I take whatever I am worried about and write it down in my prayer journal. The list usually contains four to eight worries, though one day I had fifty-seven! This is how I pray about everything. I take each item on my list and give it to God. I turn my pressure list into my prayer list. One by one I cast all my cares on Him. By doing this, I replace worry with prayer.

When I do this, simple but wonderful things occur. My pressures turn to peace. My concerns turn into confidence. My burdens are lifted. My hope is renewed, and I feel better. More important, God works on my problems as I ask Him to act.

The Perspective of Thankfulness

Pressures and problems are powerful forces that can easily pull our thinking off track. We lose perspective. Little troubles or problems that have a vague chance of becoming reality can look so massive that they crowd out God's blessings. We get so focused on a little bad that we fail to see the abundant good we have been given.

My eldest son is now in college. So I appreciate one of my favorite stories on perspective even more. It involves a daughter's letter written to her parents from college.

Dear Mom and Dad,

Just thought I'd drop you a note to clue you in on my plans. I've fallen in love with a guy named Jim. He quit high school in the eleventh grade to get married. It didn't work out, and he's been divorced now about a year. Jim and I have been going together for a few months, and we plan to get married in the fall. Until then, I decided to move into his apartment.

I hate to admit it, but I am having a problem with drugs. By the way, I think I am pregnant. At any rate, I dropped out of school last week, although I would like to finish college sometime in the future.

The young woman's parents anxiously turned over the letter to page two.

Mom and Dad, I want you to know that everything I have written so far is false. None of it is true. But it is true that I got a C– in French and that I failed a math test. I just wanted to put things in perspective.

Anxiety has a devious way of causing us to see only negatives. We tend to think about negatives from our past, are overwhelmed by the negatives currently confronting us, and are staggered by the potential negatives looming on the horizon. Gratitude has the power to shrink negatives down to size.

I have a friend named Sandy. Seizures have made her unable to work and have put her in the hospital on many occasions. Yet every time I talk to her, she gushes with gratitude. The last time we spoke, she told me her most recent seizure blocked her verbal abilities for a time. If I were in her shoes, I would be worried about what further losses I might experience, but not Sandy. She uses the power of thanksgiving to replace worry and usher in peace.

When I talked with her about her health issues, she smiled

broadly and said, "But it's a blessing." Then she really floored me. She said, "I am thankful for it because it helped me be a better listener."

As she spoke, her face shone. Her eyes sparkled with joy, and her smile radiated peace. Sandy is less than five feet tall, but I could tell I was in the presence of a spiritual giant, a very powerful person. Sandy has learned to tap fully into the power of thanksgiving. Never underestimate the power of thanksgiving, because it is the cure for worry.

I have a few lists in the back of my journal enumerating things I am thankful for. When I get anxious or down, I simply refer to these lists. This lifts me up. I generally walk away humming and thinking, "I have it better than I thought. God has been good to me."

We cannot be full of gratitude and full of worry at the same time. The only way to change strong emotions is to replace them with ones that are more powerful. The apostle Paul learned that thanksgiving has the power to eradicate worry.

Peace in the Place of Worry

The apostle Paul said, "The peace of God, which transcends all understanding, will guard your hearts and your minds in Christ Jesus" (Philippians 4:7). God promises that His peace has the power to replace our anxiety. When we give our problems to God, who is greater than our problems, we find peace that is greater than our problems. Could it be that when we fail to experience such peace, we have failed to give our problems to God in prayer?

But the beauty of prayer is not seen in how it makes us feel. The beauty of prayer is in what it does. Prayer invites God into our situation. It turns the problem over to the One who is big enough to handle it. And He handles it with peace.

I sometimes revisit my daily prayer list late at night or first thing the next morning. I do this because I often forget the worries I had listed the pervious morning. Often I find that God has already worked them out. I love to put checks by all my answered prayers. And there are many answered prayers. Some of my concerns never materialize. Some do, and God defeats them that very day. In other areas of concern, I do not see the answer, but I do see God working.

A *Final Encouragement*

Are you facing some difficult decisions, anxious situations, or tough adversaries? Stop worrying and start praying. Write down your worries. Spread them out before the Lord. Ask Him to take care of them. Then leave them with Him and go off into victory.

Notes

1. Commentary by A. R. Fausett in Jamieson, Fausett & Brown: The Epistle of Paul the Apostle to the Philippians, Blue Letter Bible, www.blueletterbible.org/tmp_dir/c/1120182378-5162.html (June 30, 2005).
2. Courson, The Epistle to the Philippians: Philippians One, Blue Letter Bible, www.blueletterbible.org/tmp_dir/c/1120183548-1988.html (June 30, 2005).
3. A. R. Fausett in Blue Letter Bible, www.blueletterbible.org/tmp_dir/c/1120182785-5695.htm (June 30, 2005).
4. Courson, in The Blue Letter Bible, www.blueletterbible.org/tmp_dir/c/1120222581-229.html (July 1, 2005).

19

God's Promise of Spiritual Revival

Isaiah 55:17

Do you ever feel spiritually lifeless? How about inwardly empty? Are you less than hot in your love relationship with God? Do you ever wish that the guilt that is keeping you from really experiencing God were wiped completely away?

Would you like to know that you are as close to God as you can be?

Years ago, an entire nation was wrestling with these sort of questions. The answers led them to experience God's promise of revival.

The Water Gate Revival

To my generation, the name Watergate dredges up memories of an ugly bruise on our nation's conscience. Many of us recall the painful period of intense national scrutiny, intrigue, and shame. Watergate is the name of a Washington, D.C., hotel, the site of a crime that led to the downfall of President Nixon. For America, Watergate signifies a national loss of confidence in its leaders.

Hundreds of years before this, an actual gate served as the backdrop for a national spiritual awakening. Around 450 BC, Nehemiah led a group of Jews from Babylon back to Jerusalem. This remnant left the confines of captivity to rebuild the city's walls. One of the twelve gates was on the east side of Jerusalem near the Gihon Spring. People carried water into the city from the spring through that gate, so it became known as the Water Gate.

The walls and buildings of the city of Jerusalem had lain in ruins for several generations because of the ineffective attempts to defend the city against foreign invaders. In spite of long odds, dangerous opposition, and constant frustration, Nehemiah and his crew successfully rebuilt the walls surrounding the city. This made it safe for the captured Hebrew remnant to begin to return and rebuild their nation.

After the walls were complete, Nehemiah gathered all of the people together in front of the Water Gate. They were excited to be safely together in the holy city. That day was especially significant because Ezra did something that had not been done for seventy years—he read the Law of God aloud to the people of God (Nehemiah 8:1–3).

It must have been an awesome scene. Ezra, the wise man of God, walked out on a raised platform carrying the law of God; carefully, lovingly, deliberately, he unrolled the scroll. A holy hush descended on the people, and with quiet spontaneity all stood as one in profound reverence to the word of God (Nehemiah 8:4–5).

I can almost hear Ezra excitedly clear his throat, then lift his voice and bless the Lord, hailing Him as the great God. I can see the people soberly nodding and answering, "Amen! Amen!" as they bow their faces to the ground in deep humility and worship (Nehemiah 8:6).

All morning Ezra read the Law. The sound of God's word cascaded over the people, some of it vaguely familiar. Although most of them had never heard it read aloud, some may have heard bits and pieces of it from their parents or grandparents. The pointed and powerful words from the Lord cut deep into the people's hearts as Ezra and other priests explained and applied them (Nehemiah 8:8).

The words of God's Law were crystal clear and convicting. The people became aware that individually and as a nation, they had disobeyed the Law. Yet the Lord had been good to them. He kept them intact during the captivity. He restored them to their homeland. He gave them back their city.

Soon, sniffling was heard throughout the gathering. Men, women, boys, and girls wiped their eyes as hot tears raced down their dusty cheeks. Sobs and weeping punctuated the scene (Nehemiah 8:9).

Those were tears of gratitude and guilt. Ezra, Nehemiah, and the other leaders cried out, "This day is sacred to the LORD your God. Do not mourn or weep" (Nehemiah 8:9). Then Ezra sent them home to get something to eat, saying, "Go and enjoy choice food and sweet drinks, and send some to those who have nothing prepared. . . . Do not grieve, for the joy of the LORD is your strength" (8:10).

The next day, as they read the Law of the Lord, they discovered that they were supposed to have been celebrating three annual weeklong feasts. These weeks were to be set apart for God. Since it was fall, they dedicated the next seven days to celebrate the Feast of Ingathering, also called the Feast of Tabernacles (Nehemiah 8:13–18; Exodus 23:16; Leviticus 23:33–36). The people celebrated with great joy (Nehemiah 8:17). Each day they continued to listen eagerly as Ezra read the Law (8:18).

The weeklong feast culminated in a sacred assembly for the confession of sins. They spent a quarter of the day listening to the Law and the next quarter confessing their sins and worshiping the Lord (Nehemiah 9:1–3). The day of confession of sins, mixed with praise and worship, culminated in all of the leaders and the people signing a covenant of strict obedience to the Law (9:38–10:39). The decisions and commitments made during this nine day revival blessed and carried the nation of Israel for years to come.

Revival

The word *revival* is a compound word combining the prefix *re-* and the Latin word *vive. Re-* means "new" or "again," and *vive* means *life.* So, *revival* is "new life" or "renewed life."

English Bibles use *revive* several times in the Old Testament. "Revive" is the translation of the Hebrew word *hayah,* which comes from the root *hay,* meaning "life." The prefix *ya* denotes "again" or "renewed."

A spiritual revival is a renewal of life to the spiritually dead. It is a return of people who are spiritually distant; a renewal of obedience to the Lord; a rekindling of a relationship with God. Years before the days of Ezra and the revival at the Water Gate, the prophet Isaiah recorded a promise of revival that applies to every generation:

> *For thus says the High and Lofty One who inhabits eternity, whose name is Holy: "I dwell in the high and holy place, with him who has a contrite and humble spirit, to revive the spirit of the humble, and to revive the heart of the contrite ones.*
>
> Isaiah 57:15 NKJV

The Source of Revival Is God

The Lord's promise is that when we dwell with Him we will experience revival. Revival is a good thing. Even more, it is a *God thing.* Revival is the return of spiritual life, and God is the

Spirit of life. When we experience God, we experience His life. When we lack God, we lack life.

God is the creator of life (Genesis 1:1). Jesus declared that He is the way, the truth, and the life (John 14:6). Since God is the source of life, He is the source of revival. As Isaiah 57:15 reminds us, revival comes from the "High and Lofty One who inhabits eternity, whose name is Holy." We cannot grit our teeth and become spiritually alive. Revival comes from God. The closer we get to God, the more alive we become.

In other words, God's part in revival is simply to be himself. Since He is life, when we get close to Him, we experience renewed spiritual life.

The Key to Revival Is Spiritual Brokenness

God is the source of revival. So how do we access that source? Look again at this promise. Note the words that are repeated there:

> *For thus says the* High *and* Lofty *One who inhabits eternity, whose name is* Holy*: "I dwell in the* high *and* holy *place, with him who has a* contrite *and* humble *spirit, to revive the spirit of the* humble*, And to revive the heart of the* contrite *ones." (emphasis added)*

The keys to this promise are found in the concepts of highness, holiness, humility, and contrition. God is high and lofty. He lives on a higher plane than anyone else. He also is holy. He dwells in the holy place. We experience Him as we humble ourselves before His highness and His holiness. In other words, the door to God is opened with the key of brokenness.

The New Testament author James wrote as though he was

very familiar with Isaiah 55:17. Note carefully his clarion call to humility in light of God's loftiness.

> *"God opposes the proud but gives grace to the humble." Submit yourselves, then, to God. Resist the devil, and he will flee from you. Come near to God and he will come near to you. Wash your hands, you sinners, and purify your hearts, you double-minded. Grieve, mourn and wail. Change your laughter to mourning and your joy to gloom. Humble yourselves before the Lord, and he will lift you up."*
>
> JAMES 4:6–10

Spiritual brokenness becomes evident as we humble ourselves and admit that we are not God, we are insufficient, we are not holy, and we need God. Then we yield to God and confess our sin, and revival is the result.

For example, the disciple Peter, after denying Jesus, returned to God with great power and preached the greatest sermon ever given. But this did not occur until after he was first broken and honest about his failure to be loyal to Christ (John 21:15–19). Next, he spent a week in the upper room, praying with 120 other believers (Acts 1:12–26). Then he was revived and stood in Jerusalem preaching the gospel to Israel (2:1–36).

The prodigal son returned to the blessed life of his father's house. But not until he came to his senses and admitted his foolishness, confessing his sin in leaving the father in the first place (Luke 15:11–24).

Paul lived in a continual state of revival because he was spiritually broken. On one hand, he knew that without Christ he was the chief of sinners (1 Timothy 1:15). On the other, he could do all things through Christ (Philippians 4:13)

Remember, when we finally come to the end of ourselves, we come to the beginning of God. Spiritual brokenness is the key that opens the door to God's revival.

A Final Encouragement

Have you grown tired of what you can do? Are you weary with the status quo? Are you worn out by business as usual? Are you sick of human-sized things? Do you hunger for some God-sized things? Do you long to see God do in seconds what you have failed to do over years? Is good enough no longer good enough? If you have reached this place of humble honesty, you are on the verge of revival.

God cannot resist the spiritually broken. He gives them spiritual revival. He has done it for many others, and He'll gladly do it for you.

20 God's Promise of Divine Protection

PSALM 91:1–2

Have you ever felt a strange heaviness of spirit or oppression in your mind that made prayer impossible? For sure, prayer can be difficult sometimes. But have you ever felt as if your prayers were shut up in a box, strangely thwarted, going nowhere, unheard? At such times, you may find that wicked, even vile thoughts rise up from nowhere. Sleep is difficult. Suicide may come to mind.

Well, you are not alone.

Chuck Swindoll says that these are "subtle yet distinct hints that evil forces are at work." He testifies, "My wife and I have often talked about how we can sense the invisible presence of the adversary."[1]

Please take note: Some weird wacko didn't say this. Chuck Swindoll is the former president of the Dallas Theological Seminary and a best-selling author. Plus, I have experienced the same things on more than one occasion. I know what it is like to come under spiritual attack. And you do, too, although maybe you may not realize what it is or know what to do about it.

When I first began to pursue God, Satan came after me. I began to experience spiritual attack, not unlike what Swindoll described. I thought I was the only one experiencing this. I wondered if I was crazy. Eventually I discovered that it is not unusual for the enemy to attack us when we step out for God.

But back then I had no idea what it was or what to do about it. In fact, I was so intimidated that I drew back from my pursuit of God and postponed getting radical in my walk with God. The enemy was successful. His attacks were effective. I was defeated.

Under Attack in AD 1500

Martin Luther was a monk, a theologian, and one of the most influential people in history. His insistence on salvation by grace sparked a movement called the Protestant Reformation and led to the rise of Protestantism. His love of music and hymns brought a renaissance to church music. His ideologies helped shape several European governments. He may have done more for God than anyone else in his day, and the enemy did not like it.

Luther believed in a literal devil and the attack of evil spirits. He freely spoke of being pestered by devils, evil spirits, and demons throughout his life. These attacks increased in frequency and intensity when he went into hiding in Wartburg Castle. There Luther, a fugitive for his faith, spent his time translating the Bible into the language of his people, German.

God's enemy was aware of the power that would be unleashed when the Bible became available in the language of the masses. Satan did not like this and kept attacking Luther. One night the attacks hit a climax. Luther sensed the presence of the enemy in his room. Exasperated by the close and constant hounding, Martin whirled and heaved his inkwell at the devil. The ink stain on the wall in Wartburg Castle was visible for centuries.

I am not sure how effective his inkwell was in defeating the devil, but I do know that Luther's usual practice of praising, praying, and trusting in God's promises is effective. Later in life, Luther put into practice God's promise of deliverance when under attack. He penned a song. I am sure you have sung this hymn, but I bet you probably never noticed how clearly the words speak to those under enemy attack.

A mighty fortress is our God,
A bulwark never failing;
Our helper He, amid the flood
Of mortal ills prevailing.
For still our ancient foe
Ooth seek to work us woe;
His craft and pow'r are great,
And, armed with cruel hate,
On earth is not his equal.

Did we in our own strength confide,
Our striving would be losing;
Were not the right Man on our side,
The man of God's own choosing.
Dost ask who that may be?
Christ Jesus, it is He;
Lord Sabaoth His name,
From age to age the same,
And He must win the battle.

And though this world, with devils filled,
Should threaten to undo us,
We will not fear, for God hath willed
His truth to triumph through us.
The Prince of Darkness grim,
We tremble not for him;

His rage we can endure,
For lo, his doom is sure;
One little word shall fell him.[2]

Under Attack in 1990

When we first started our church, I was ignorant of the enemy's schemes, and the enemy took advantage of that. Every Saturday evening was miserable at my house, especially if a big crowd was expected on Sunday morning. The kids would be healthy all week, but wake up vomiting in the middle of Saturday night. Or they would be good all week, but get in arguments and fights with each other on Saturday night. Or my wife and I would get along great all week and find ourselves getting upset with each other over some insignificant thing on Saturday night. Also, at about 12:30 a.m. every Saturday night, after we had fallen asleep, the phone would ring. It would be either a wrong number or a drunk.

I may seem a little slow, but after a few years of this, I began to see a pattern. So I took action. First, I made an effort to read my Bible and pray aloud before retiring on Saturday night. Second, swallowing my pride one Sunday night, I explained to my congregation what was going on and asked them to pray for me every Saturday night. The next Saturday night was heaven in my home. The kids were good and healthy; Cathy and I got along great; the phone did not ring; I slept like a baby; and that Sunday I preached better than ever.

I have shared this story at pastors' conferences and have had many pastors and their wives tell me afterward, often with tears in their eyes, how they, too, have had to battle the enemy on Saturday nights. Many of them wanted me to know that they had discovered God's promise of deliverance:

He who dwells in the shelter of the Most High will rest in the shadow of the Almighty. I will say of the LORD, "He is my refuge and my fortress, my God, in whom I trust."

PSALM 91:1–2

God is a supernaturally strong shelter. He is a formidable fortress and a haven of true rest. We do not have to fear when the enemy assaults us. We can be protected. We also don't have to fight back, and we don't need to surrender to defeat. We need to learn to dwell in the shelter of the Most High and rest in the shadow of the Almighty.

The Lord is described in this promise as "the Most High" and "the Almighty." This means that He is higher, bigger, smarter, and stronger than the enemy and so able to defeat him. The name "Most High" (in Hebrew, *El Elyon*) means "the God above all gods." If anyone has the authority to keep promises, God does. The name "Almighty" (in Hebrew, *El Shaddai*), means "the God who sees and provides." God knows when we are attacked and is able to rescue us from it. He is willing and able to protect us from enemy assault. He is greater than our foe. As the apostle John wrote, "You, dear children, are from God and have overcome them, because the one who is in you is greater than the one who is in the world" (1 John 4:4).

Accessing Divine Deliverance

God will, of course, do His part. But we must learn to do ours. Psalm 91 points to several doors of entry to the fortress of our Father God.

- *Make Yourself at Home in God*

> *He who* dwells *in the shelter of the Most High will rest in the shadow of the Almighty.*
>
> PSALM 91:1 (EMPHASIS ADDED)

We must make ourselves at home in God, and God will make Himself at home in us. Protection is within a relationship with God. You need to get in God and dwell there.

- *Trust the Lord Actively*

> *I will say of the LORD, "He is my refuge and my fortress, my God, in whom I* trust.*"*
>
> PSALM 91:2 (EMPHASIS ADDED)

We must have faith not only that He'll one day take us to heaven. We need to rely on him to protect us from enemy attack. We cannot defeat the enemy or handle the attack on our own. We must depend on the Lord.

Every time the enemy begins to assault you with worrisome thoughts, tell God that He is your refuge. When you are hit with floods of fear, declare that God is your fortress. When troubles come, proclaim your trust in God.

- *Love the Lord Loyally*

> *"Because he loves me," says the LORD, "I will rescue him; I will protect him, for he acknowledges my name."*
>
> PSALM 91:14

The path to protection lies in the power of our personal relationship with the all-powerful God. If the enemy sees you using his attacks as an excuse to draw closer to God, he will be foolish to persist. Every time Satan hits you with an attack, respond by sending up praise to God.

Our hearts and minds need to be so full of God that the enemy has no room to attack and no basis of operation. The more our lives are under His authority, the less power the enemy will have to harass us.

- *Call upon the Lord Dependently*

He will call upon me, and I will answer him; I will be with him in trouble, I will deliver him and honor him.

PSALM 91:15

When you sense the enemy striking out at you, cry out to God, pray, and ask Him to protect you. Before you go to bed, call on God. When you wake up with a nightmare, call on God. When you find yourself in an argument that is becoming unreasonable, call on God. When you are oppressed with despair, call on God. When you are overwhelmed with suicidal thoughts, call on God. When temptation is all around, call on God. When evil thoughts are flooding your mind, call on God. When circumstances are eerily against you or when the atmosphere is strangely tense, call on God.

One day a dad was picking up his little girl from Sunday school. He asked her what she had learned that day. The small child gave a very insightful response: "I learned that there is a devil. When he knocks on my door, I need to ask Jesus to answer it."

A *Final Encouragement*

It's inevitable—the enemy will try to knock you off stride. But have no fear, because God is near and will deliver you. He has done it many times for many others; you can count on Him to do it for you.

Notes

1. Charles Swindoll, *Living Beyond the Daily Grind, Book 2: Reflections on the Songs and Sayings in Scripture* (Nashville: W Publishing Group, 1989), 260.
2. Martin Luther, "A Mighty Fortress Is Our God."

21

God's Promise of Heavenly Help

PSALM 46:1

A prayer to be said
when the world has gotten you down,
and you feel rotten,
and you're too doggone tired to pray,
and you're in a big hurry,
and besides, you're mad at everyone. . .
Help!

Ah, poster theology. Sometimes nothing says it any better. I try to be a man of prayer. Many days I pray for more than an hour at a time. I have even written a few books on prayer. But the prayer I pray most often is that one simple word, "Help!"

Many times I need divine assistance, angelic aid, real-life relief, and heavenly help. You do, too. Thankfully, there is a source for surefire supernatural support. It is expressed in Psalm 46:1, one of the most encouraging and oft-repeated promises in the Bible:

> *God is our refuge and strength, an ever-present* help *in trouble.*
>
> PSALM 46:1 (EMPHASIS ADDED)

God is a safe place to hide. He is always ready to help us. He is an ever-present, willing source of strength. He promises mercy and grace to help in time of need. Wow! Those are very encouraging promises.

When I am in seasons of severe hardship, I need all the mercy, grace, and help I can get. Thank God for His promises—like this one:

> *Let us then approach the throne of grace with confidence, so that we may receive mercy and find grace to* help *us in our time of need.*
>
> HEBREWS 4:16 (EMPHASIS ADDED)

Notice that at the beginning of Hebrews 4:16, God's help comes because we confidently approach His throne of grace and ask for it. In other words, God doesn't help those who help themselves. He helps those who ask for it.

David Asked for Help and Got It

Like you and me, David needed help many times. When his failures opened the door to inner turmoil and enemy attack, he prayed, "Come quickly to help me, O Lord my Savior" (Psalm 38:22). When swallowed by his circumstances as though in a muddy pit, he cried, "Be pleased, O LORD, to save me; O LORD, come quickly to help me" (40:13). When captured by his enemies, he prayed, "Hasten, O God, to save me; O LORD, come quickly to help me" (70:1). Later he testified, "My enemies will turn back when I call for help. By this I will know that God is for me" (56:9).

In his twilight years, David looked back on the importance of the Lord's help. A rousing song was the result:

> *If the LORD had not been on our side—let Israel say—if the LORD had not been on our side when men attacked us, when their anger flared against us, they would have swallowed us alive; the flood would have engulfed us, the torrent would have swept over us, the raging waters would have swept us away. Praise be to the LORD, who has not let us be torn by their teeth. We have escaped like a bird out of the fowler's snare; the snare has been broken, and we have escaped. Our* help *is in the name of the LORD, the Maker of heaven and earth.*
>
> PSALM 124:1–8 (EMPHASIS ADDED)

Jonah Asked for Help and Got It

Sometimes we need help because of our own ignorant rebellion. God told Jonah to go to Nineveh to preach a message of repentance. But Jonah didn't like the people of Nineveh and refused to go. Instead, he jumped on a ship headed in the opposite direction. As we know, you can run from God, but you cannot hide.

The Lord sent a ferocious storm. Jonah knew that as long as he stayed on the boat, the crew was in danger. So he had them throw him in the angry waves. As the furious sea swallowed him, Jonah asked for help, and God had an answer. Later he recalled his prayer and God's answer:

> *In my distress I called to the LORD, and he answered me. From the depths of the grave I called for* help, *and you listened to my cry. You hurled me into the deep, into the very heart of the seas, and the currents swirled about me; all your waves and breakers swept over me. . . . The engulfing waters threatened me, the deep surrounded me;*

seaweed was wrapped around my head. To the roots of the mountains I sank down; the earth beneath barred me in forever. But you brought my life up from the pit, O LORD my God.

JONAH 2:1–6 (EMPHASIS ADDED)

God promises to help his people when they ask for it. The Lord helped Jonah before he drowned by sending a giant fish to swallow him. The fish vomited the repentant prophet on the beach. Jonah immediately journeyed to Nineveh and preached to the people. Gloriously, the entire population of the city turned to the Lord.

Daniel Asked for Help and Got It

The elderly prophet Daniel was a wise, godly man in an ungodly environment. Jealous underlings were aware that Daniel regularly prayed to the Lord. They were jealous of Daniel's position of authority over them, so they set a trap for him. They tricked the king into signing a petition stating that for a thirty-day period, anyone found praying to any god other than the king would be executed in a den of lions. No exceptions were allowed. Then they waited and watched Daniel's house (see Daniel 6:1–28).

Daniel was unmoved by the new law. He knelt down and prayed to the Lord as he had always done. The conspirators caught him. But not before he asked the Lord for help.

Then these men went as a group and found Daniel praying and asking God for help.

DANIEL 6:11 (EMPHASIS ADDED)

The Lord answers when people ask for help. God heard Daniel's prayer and sprang to the rescue, sparing him from the lions. Later Daniel described the event, saying,

> *"My God sent his angel, and he shut the mouths of the lions. They have not hurt me, because I was found innocent in his sight. Nor have I ever done any wrong before you, O king."*
>
> Daniel 6:22

The king, relieved by this miraculous display of heavenly help, removed Daniel from the lethal lion's den. Daniel did not suffer even a scratch from the deadly man-eaters. Then the king had Daniel's conspirators thrown into the lions' den to see how they'd fair. Unfortunately for them, their gods were not as helpful as Daniel's had been.

> *And before they reached the floor of the den, the lions overpowered them and crushed all their bones.*
>
> Daniel 6:24

But that's not all. God's supernatural support continued flowing on behalf of Daniel and his cause.

> *Then King Darius wrote to all the peoples, nations and men of every language throughout the land: "May you prosper greatly! I issue a decree that in every part of my kingdom people must fear and reverence the God of Daniel. For he is the living God and he endures forever; his kingdom will not be destroyed, his dominion will never end. He rescues and he saves; he performs signs and*

wonders in the heavens and on the earth. He has rescued Daniel from the power of the lions." So Daniel prospered during the reign of Darius.

DANIEL 6:25–28

I guess so! God not only helped Daniel by sparing him from the lions but also aided him by eradicating his jealous conspirators. On top of that, the Lord used the king to give a tremendous testimony to the nation and to protect His people's freedom to worship Him.

Asa Asked for Help and Got It

Asa was the righteous king of Judah. God blessed his obedience, and the nation prospered. Then one dark day Zerah, a fierce warrior, marched on Judah, leading an army of one million Ethiopians and three hundred gleaming chariots. Asa faced a skilled opponent who had him outnumbered by over four hundred thousand troops *and* three hundred chariots! Judah had no defense against the awesome speed and power of the best weapons of mass destruction on the planet in 900 BC. This could have been one of the most massive massacres in history.

Asa did the right thing. He asked for help, resting on God's promise.

Then Asa called to the LORD his God and said, "LORD, there is no one like you to help *the powerless against the mighty. Help us, O LORD our God, for we rely on you, and in your name we have come against this vast army. O LORD, you are our God; do not let man prevail against you."*

2 CHRONICLES 14:11 (EMPHASIS ADDED)

God keeps His promises. The Lord heard Asa's prayer and gave him a miraculous answer:

> *The LORD struck down the Cushites before Asa and Judah. The Cushites fled, and Asa and his army pursued them as far as Gerar. Such a great number of Cushites fell that they could not recover; they were crushed before the LORD and his forces. The men of Judah carried off a large amount of plunder. They destroyed all the villages around Gerar, for the terror of the LORD had fallen upon them. They plundered all these villages, since there was much booty there. They also attacked the camps of the herdsmen and carried off droves of sheep and goats and camels. Then they returned to Jerusalem.*
>
> 1 CHRONICLES 14:12–15

Don't miss all that the Lord did in helping Asa and his people. First, God sent a supernatural dread upon Zerah's army, the Cushites. We do not know how He did it, but we know that He did. They fled in fear before the battle began. As a result, all Asa and his men had to do was chase them down. Miraculously, the huge Ethiopian war machine was completely conquered by Asa's smaller army.

But beyond this, Asa's men gathered sensational spoils. As they hunted down the fleeing Ethiopians, they pillaged the Philistine villages that had aided them as they ran away. On top of that, they defeated and robbed the camps of the nomadic herdsmen who had been supplying the Cushite army with sheep, goats, and camels. So Asa and Judah not only did not get crushed; they won the battle without losing a man and got an incredible amount of plunder in the process! Yay, God!

A *Final Encouragement*

You are human, so you will always need help. God is the best source of the best help. He helped David, Jonah, Daniel, Asa, and countless others. And if you ask, He has promised to help you.

22

Final Thoughts

A mother came home from shopping and found her freshly baked pie dug out crudely in the center. A gooey spoon lay in the sink, and crumbs were scattered over the kitchen counter and floor.

She called her son into the kitchen. "Son," she said sternly, "you promised me you wouldn't touch that pie before dinner."

The boy hung his head.

"And I promised you I'd spank you if you did," she continued.

Her son's face brightened. "Now that I've broken my promise," he offered, "it's okay with me if you break yours, too!"

Maybe you have read this book with skepticism. You are thinking, "I have asked, but I have not received. I believed God was working all for good, but things just keep getting worse. I cried out to God for help, but there is no help in sight."

I know exactly how you are feeling. As a student of the promises, I have discovered a few truths that apply to those rare occasions when God seems silent.

- *God is not merely a machinelike "blessing dispenser."* He is our heavenly Father. He deeply desires to build a relationship with us. His desire is that His blessings build up and flow out of our relationship with Him.

- *God is always more committed to His cause and our character than to our comfort or convenience.* He will often trade our immediate pleasure for our long-term profit and His kingdom's progress. He is very willing to suspend our relief in order to test and deepen our belief.

- *Just as it takes faith to claim a promise, it requires faith to hang on to it when it seems to be ineffective.* God richly honors such resilient faith. If you need to be convinced about this, read Hebrews 11:35–40.

- *God is very patient.* He will frequently withhold a small blessing today in order to prepare us to receive a larger blessing tomorrow. He will not give us pretty good blessings now in lieu of really great blessings later.

- *God's ways are not necessarily our ways.* Some events will only make sense years from now. Some situations will remain foggy until we can see with heavenly eyes.

- *The Lord is the sovereign God.* He has the authority and power to do whatever He wants, however, whenever, and wherever He wants to do it.

- *God is always faithful, even when we are faithless.*

- *Ultimately, you can never go wrong by trusting God.*

A Promise Kept

A year ago, I was working on the first book in this series. It is called *The 21 Most Effective Prayers in the Bible.* As I wrote that book, I consistently applied the thirteenth promise in this book, God's promise of answered prayer. I asked specifically that God would bless that book in larger ways than I envisioned. I prayed that it would encourage thousands of people to become more effective in prayer.

I believed that the Lord would answer my prayer and keep His promise, unless He had a good reason not to. Then, in the busyness of life, I forgot about it.

A few weeks ago, I walked into one of the largest bookstore chains in the nation. As I usually do, I headed toward the Christian Inspiration section. I began to look through books according to their alphabetical listing. What I often do is try to picture a book with my name on it sitting on the shelves. I read over the books written by people with last names beginning with the letters *A, B, C,* and *D.* I wondered if I would ever have a book in such a large bookstore chain.

Then I came to the *E*s and was stunned. Leading off the *E* section was a book by Dave Earley. I gasped and then smiled. Pulling the cell phone out of my pocket, I dialed my wife.

"Hello, Cathy," I said as calmly as possible. "Guess where I am."

"I have no idea," she said. "Where are you?"

"I am in the bookstore. Guess what I'm looking at?"

"A book?" she asked wisely. "I don't know," she continued, "what are you looking at?"

"I am looking at *my* book! *The 21 Most Effective Prayers in the Bible* is on the shelf."

"Are you going to buy it?" she asked.

"No," I said. "Then I wouldn't have a book in this bookstore, and besides, I already have a copy."

As I hung up, I sensed God speaking to my heart. "Why are you so surprised?" He asked. "Didn't you expect Me to keep My promise?"

A *Final Encouragement*

There are over seven thousand promises in God's Word. We've looked at twenty-one of the most encouraging ones. I am sure that you can grab hold of a few of these and claim them as your own. God is big enough to keep every one of His promises. He loves you and longs to bless you. Keep your eyes on Him and continue to trust Him to keep His Word. Then when He answers your prayers, He'll be able to ask you as He did me, "Didn't you expect me to keep my promise?"

Also from Barbour Publishing

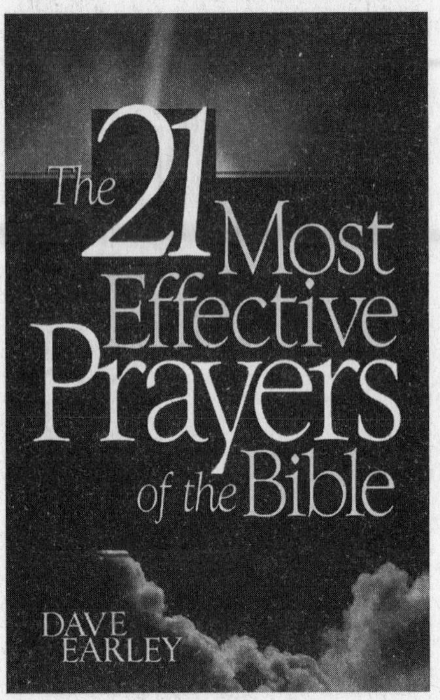

The 21 Most Effective Prayers of the Bible

Speaks to believers of all ages, backgrounds, and maturity levels with an uplifting message: that the prayers of the Bible are prayers for us today. Not an exhaustive, scholarly study, this very readable volume investigates twenty-one heartfelt prayers that produced results.

ISBN 1-59310-605-X

$8.97